AF568135

Industrial Development and World Trade Organisation

INDUSTRIAL DEVELOPMENT AND WORLD TRADE ORGANISATION

By
Dr. M. Lakshmi Narasaiah
M.A., Ph.D.
Professor of Economics,
Coordinator, Department of M.B.A.
Sri Krishnadevaraya University Post-graduate Centre,
Kurnool–518 002
Andhra Pradesh (India)

DISCOVERY PUBLISHING HOUSE
NEW DELHI

First Published–2005

ISBN: 81-7141-941-0

Published by:

DISCOVERY PUBLISHING HOUSE

4831/24, Prahlad Street, Ansari Road, Darya Ganj
New Delhi–110 002 (India)
Phone: 23279245, • Fax: 91-11-23253475
e-mail: dphtemp@indiatimes.com

Printed at:

Amit Enterprises, Delhi

Preface

When trade policies are discussed nationally or internationally people as consumers are largely forgotten. Despite their numbers, they do not carry the weight that producers and other lobbies command. Individually, consumers are seldom informed about how the availability, quality, price and choice of the hundreds of items which they buy in the shops each year are affected by trade policy decisions. If they know how much of their household budgets are determined by decisions to protect individual industries and for how little effect they might be shocked.

Equally, when it is debated publicly, the benefits that would fall to the consumer are usually ignored. This brief study is an attempt to put the consumer interest squarely in the public arena.

How Do Government Decisions on Trade Affect the Consumer?

Virtually all-protective policies mean higher prices for the consumer. And if it is not a consumer who pays, it will be domestic producer. These are some of the main actions taken by national authorities.

Governments frequently and for the most part, legally raise revenue and protect domestic industries by imposing duties on imported products. If a product has a 25 per cent tariff, the price in the shop will normally be 25 per cent more than its price at the port or airport.

Global quotas and other numerical limits on imports are sometimes legal sometimes not. Either way the intention is to restrict access to the market in such a away that domestic producers of the same product can raise their prices without being forced out of business through lack of competitiveness. Quotas are frequently preferred by those demanding protection because the impact on prices is less obvious than with a tariff. Once again, prices go up in the shops and limits may be so narrow that goods disappear from the shelves altogether.

Voluntary export restraints are quotas of an even more costly kind for the importing country. They allow foreign suppliers to charge higher prices than would be possible under a tariff or normal quota. By "bribing" the exporter this way, opposition to the protection is reduced.

Subsidies are sometimes paid to domestic producers to help them compete with import competition by keeping their costs artificially low. This keeps prices down. Unfortunately, the consumer as a tax payer ends up paying for the subsidy. In so doing, he is prevented from keeping more of his income to spend on other goods, which may be produced by more efficient industries. One thing is sure once industries get used to subsidies, it is very hard to wean then away.

Rules permit governments to impose extra duties on imports where products are shown to be dumped (sold below the normal price in the exporting country) or subsidised, and where the effect of dumping or subsidisation is demonstrated to damage the corresponding domestic industry. While these duties may be justified, they nevertheless always serve to raise the price for consumers to knock products completely out of the market. Yet very few, if any, countries give much weight to consumer interest when deciding whether to impose such penalty duties. And their use has grown disturbingly in recent years.

Governments usually impose standards of safety, quality, public health and environmental protection for good reasons often in the interests of consumers. Sometimes, however, the standards and the procedures which enforce them are no more than hidden protection for domestic producers. In imposing unnecessary measures on imports, governments penalize consumers through higher prices and the non-availability of goods.

Dr. M. Lakshmi Narasaiah

Contents

1

Technological Entrepreneurship:

The New Force for Economic Growth

Entrepreneurship has emerged as a major new force for change. The dynamic role of modern small business in economic growth has received fresh recognition worldwide. It is essential to promote entrepreneurship and to mobilize the dynamism of the private sector for accelerated national development. An unbridled private sector may not, however, ensure growth with equity. It is the prime responsibility of governments to create policy frameworks that enable businesses to apply technology for competitive advantage and for the well-being of the public.

The Changing Global Environment

As agents of change and progress, entrepreneurs start by identifying a market opportunity and matching this with social or technical innovations. They then proceed to mobilize the resources necessary to drive their business concept to its commercial realisation. The development of a product or service with a high technology content—never easy anywhere, or at today's rapidly changing global environment. It calls for restructuring the available technology and business development systems and developing the skills needed by a new breed of "techno-entrepreneurs" to transform innovations into market opportunities at home and abroad. It also requires reorienting the present processes and priorities of technical and economic cooperation among countries.

Amidst the global concerns of environmental preservation, poverty elimination and social development, the practical problems of entrepreneurship are not being properly addressed, even though entrepreneurs will create the bulk of enterprises, jobs and wealth.

A torrent of technology-based goods hits the market every week, ostensibly improving the quality of our lives while simultaneously creating complexity and dislocation. The pace of progress in information technologies, microelectronics, robotics, new materials, biomedical sciences, space science and other advanced technologies quickens, significantly changing the way we live. The growth of markets for these technologies also proceeds apace.

Further, technological change is taking place today against a background of growing intra-national and international disequilibria. While the transformation from State-centred to market-oriented development is opening up enormous opportunities and options, it has also caused severe short-term hardships. In order to survive and prosper in these changing times, India and its enterprises need enlightened government policies, good technical infrastructure and strong cultural roots.

Traditional production factors are giving way to a new paradigm characterized by new patterns of trade, investment and employment, and by informal networking life-long learning and technological entrepreneurship. The manufacturing sector in India continues to be dominated by food products, textiles, chemicals and other traditional industry, mainly in the public sector. However, change is coming, albeit slowly. State enterprises are being corporatized pending privatisation, and the share of knowledge-based and information-related activities in the marketplace is rising perceptibly. Restructuring policies now place emphasis (often purely rhetorical) on the role of the private sector. The legacy of decades of centrally planned development is generally inimical to private enterprise. In turn, the private sector has been slow to respond to economic liberalisation in India and generally failed to generate the new employment necessary to absorb new entrants to the labour force.

The regulatory problems of an onerous tax structure and administration, poor access to finance and raw materials, over-regulation of labour and land use, pervasive bureaucracy and restricted markets have been significant barriers to entrepreneurial growth.

Towards Competitive Performance

The imperative of improved performance has serious implications for India if it is to survive, stay abreast and succeed. It calls for national efforts on systemic efficiency and productivity growth, the move from an investment-driven to an innovation-driven economy and sustained higher-order competitiveness; towards enhanced customer satisfaction at home and penetration of selected markets abroad. Concurrently, governments and business have to address such intractable problems as poverty, corruption and the degradation of the environment.

Creating New Technology-Based Ventures

Starting a new business in India is a hazardous task. Problems are compounded when the venture is technology-based:

- Capital requirements are generally larger, while traditional banks are ill equipped to process the perceived risk. Venture capital generally only becomes as option when the venture has documented the merits of its management, market and innovation.
- Knowledge-based ventures can benefit form linkages to sources of knowledge—e.g. the technical university or research lab. Such mentoring needs to be cultivated.
- Techno-entrepreneurs often have technical skills but usually lack the business management and marketing skills necessary for success. These need to be supplemented.
- In fields where technology is changing rapidly, it is often advantageous to make technology-acquisition arrangements. Souring such innovations, negotiating technology licensing agreements and protecting the intellectual property itself require special skills.

- Knowledge-based innovations are inherently more risky than others. The management of this unique risk requires assessment techniques and vision.
- Technology-based ventures often have social and environmental implications, which need to be managed carefully.
- Penetrating a competitive market requires good market intelligence, a good strategic plan and good luck.

Special Characteristics of "Techno-Entrepreneurs"

The popular misconceptions are that techno-entrepreneurs are born, not made; that they take risks with other people's money and fail more often than they succeeded. In fact, entrepreneur skills can be identified and developed. The entrepreneur is typically an innovator who formulates new solutions to existing problems, mobilizes resources and stimulates others to participate in his or her team. These aptitudes develop over time, often starting in childhood, as the person faces new challenges and learns from failure.

Entrepreneurial opportunities can be founds in every industrializing country, community and family. Principal sources of entrepreneurs for knowledge-based ventures are often the university and government research laboratories, the large industrial and military establishments and professional service firms. Some motivations of the entrepreneur are the need to: be independent; create value; contribute to society; earn recognition; become rich or; quite often, simply not to be unemployed. Value-adding ventures with good growth potential can best be developed in an open market and in a culture, which supports risk-taking.

The techno-entrepreneur anywhere has the challenge of moving a concept through the prototype and production phases towards creation of a product which market needs at a price consistent with the value created and with the ability of customers to pay.

Equally important, the market itself has to be developed and sustained. It is not enough to be first with a better mousetrap if one does not have the skills to educate and reach potential buyers and to set the market standard.

Hence one has to distinguish between innovators and inventors. The inventor is typically a creative person in a quest for knowledge or for producing new products, without determining in advance whether a real market exists for his or her inventions. On the other hand, the innovator draws on existing knowledge and the talents of others to develop or adapt a product or service at a volume and cost that can capture a significant portion of an identified market. The flexibility and creativity of a small entrepreneurial techno-venture may lead to more incremental and break-through innovations than can be generated by larger-sized firms in many sectors.

The pace and pattern of India's economic development now depend in large measure on its technical resource base. In this context, the key determinants are the skills to apply technology for enhanced competitiveness, as well as to create techbased ventures. Techno-entrepreneurs have to be supported by appropriate national structures and international linkages if they are to survive and flourish in an intensely competitive world.

2

The Biggest Industry the World has Ever Seen:

The Future of World Tourism

The year 2020 will see the penetration of technology into all aspects of life. It will become possible to live one's days without exposure to other people, according to WTO's latest look into the future.

But this bleak prognosis has a silver lining for the tourism sector. People in the high-tech future will crave the human touch and tourism will be the principal means to achieve this.

Tourism companies that manage to provide "high-touch" products will prosper. Upscale, luxury sevices that pamper and spoil their customers have a bright future in the upcoming century, but WTO's report also predicts good prospects for low-budget destinations and packages. Self-catering holiday facilities, for example, which offer plenty of opportunities for socializing among families and friends. Opportunities abound at both ends of the spectrum and there will be plenty of them.

$5 Billion a Day Industry

WTO's Study Tourism: 2020 Vision predicts 1.5. billion tourists will be visiting foreign countries annually by the year 2020, spending more that US$2 trillion—or US$5 billion every day. These forecasts represent nearly three times more international tourists than the 66m million recorded in 1999 and nearly five times more tourism spending, which last year topped US$453 billion. Tourist arrivals are predicted to grow by an average 4.3 per cent a year over the next two decades, while receipts from international tourism will climb by 6.7 per cent a year.

To factor in domestic tourism, WTO multiplies arrivals by 10 and quadruples receipts, which brings us to the grant totals of 16 billion tourists spending US$8 trillion in 2020.

Tourism in the 21st century will not only be the world's biggest industry, it will be the largest by far that the world has ever seen. Along with its phenomenal growth and size, the tourism industry will also have to take on more responsibility for its extensive impacts. Not only its economic impact, but also its impact on the environment, on societies and on cultural sites, all of which will be increasingly scrutinized by governments, consumer groups and the travelling public.

We hope that Tourism 2020 Vision will be more than a useful marketing tool, that it will act as a warning signal for destinations—helping them recognize the need to prepare for the pressure of growth, WTO is advising destinations to implement long-term, strategic planning and to strengthen the partnerships, both strategically and at the operational level, between the public and private sectors.

Growth of Long-haul

Tourism: 2020 Vision indicates that tourists of the 21st century will be travelling further afield on their holidays, often to China and even to outer space. The percentage of long-haul travel is predicted to increase from 18 per cent in 1995 to 24 per cent by 2020.

Tourism companies looking to cash in on this booming sector are advised to look towards Asia. China will be the world's number one destination by the year 2020 and it will also become the fourth most important generating market. Currently it does not even figure among the world's destinations predicted to make great strides in the tourism industry are Russia, Hong Kong, Thailand, Singapore, Indonesia and South Africa.

Short pleasure voyages to outer space will become a reality by 2004 or 2005, according to the study carried out by WTO Statistics Chief Enzo Paci in consultation with 85 governments and 50 tourism visionaries.

It is expected space trips will last up to four days and cost on average US$100,000. NASA, the US space agency, has recently surveyed the travel industry for interest in space tourism and some US companies are already taking reservations and deposits from private citizens hoping to become the first tourists in outer space.

But while some travellers may be suiting up for space voyages, the vast majority of the world's populations will never leave their own countries, not even by the year 2020.

Only 7 per cent of the world's population will be travelling internationally by the year 2020, up from 3.5 per cent in 1996-but still just the tip of the ice berg.

European Trends

"Tourism: 2020 Vision" predicts that Europe will remain by far the leading inbound tourism region as well as the main generator of international tourists. International arrivals in Europe will reach 717 million by 2020? more than twice as many as last year.

Overall, tourism to Europe is predicted to grow more slowly than the world average; at a rate of 3.1 per cent annually, though some countries will fare better than others. Central and Eastern European countries will become the new motor for Europe, feeding and being fed by other European and long haul generating markets. Tourism to Central and Eastern Europe will grow by 4.8 per cent a year the former Soviet Block countries will surpass 200 million arrivals by 2016—a doubling in last 15 years.

The Eastern Mediterranean countries of Cyprus, Turkey and Israel are also expected to show good growth of 4.6 per cent a year. Tourism to the United Kingdom is forecast to grow by 4 per cent annually, just under the world average. Reflecting world patterns and increasing air travel, Europeans will be taking trips more frequently and further from home. Total outbound travel from European countries is predicted to reach 771 million trips a year by 2010, again more than twice as many as last year.

Long-haul travel to countries outside of Europe will grow by 6.1 per cent a year in the upcoming decades to reach 15 per cent of all trips taken by Europeans or 115,600,000 departures. Long-haul currently accounts for 12 per cent of European outbound travel or about 42 million trips a year.

Since the typical European tourist who spends his holiday at the beach will be more frequently choosing Asian or Caribean resorts, European beach destinations are advised to orientate their product development and marketing increasingly to new tourist sources, especially Japan, the newly industrialized countries of Asia and the America.

Mature European destinations will have continually to strive to seek product and market differentiation to avoid a tired or stale image in major generating markets.

Recipe for Success

While growth of the tourism industry will be unstoppable in the 21st century, increased benefits cannot be taken for granted. Competition among destinations will also become increasingly fierce.

The study Tourism: 2020 Vision outlines a series of 12 megatrends that will shape the sector and offers advice on how to better compete. No destination or tourism operator can afford to sit back and wait for more tourists to arrive. They have to be won—and there will be winners and losers. To be a winner, there are a number of imperatives:

1. Development focused on quality and sustainability
2. Value-for- money.
3. Full utilisation of information technology to identify and communicate effectively with market segments and niches.

Product development and marketing will need to match each other more closely, based on the main travel motivators of the 21st century. Tourism: 2020 Vision calls these motivating factors the Three E's—Entertainment, Excitement and Education.

The study also highlights the importance of image in a tourist's selection of a holiday destination in the future. While an image of safety and security is already an important deciding factor for tourists, holiday makers of the 21st century will be looking for places with a trendy image.

As 2020 Vision points out, the next century will mark the emergence the tourism destination as 'a fashion accessory'. The choice of holiday destination will help define the identity of the travellers and, in a increasingly homogeneous world, set him apart from the hordes of other tourists.

Boutique destinations and space agencies beware! You are on the threshold meeting the 21st century tourist.

3

World Trade–The Next Challenge

On 15 December 1993 the world changed. My be not as dramatically as the moment when the Berlin Wall fell, but then unlike that very necessary demolition job, the success of the Uruguay Round was a work of construction. Like the destruction of the wall, though, its effects will be profound and lasting ones felt far beyond its immediate context. It will be seen as a defining moment in modern history.

The importance of the Round can be seen in terms of boost it gives to job creation; to development; to investment; to economic reform; to the rule of law and in many other ways besides. All of these benefits are real and important. But the true value of the whole is much, much more than the sum of these parts.

Put simply, governments came to the conclusion that the notion of a new world order was not merely attractive but absolutely vital; that the reality of the global market– whatever ambitions some of them may retain for regional Integration– required a level of multilateral cooperation never before attempted.

No Losers in The Round

It has created a revolutionary framework for economic, legal and political cooperation. But now turn to the immediate results of the Round. Seeing them as a profit and loss account or a scorecard of winners and losers is to see them in static terms, as one-off conclusions with finite effects. This misses the point completely.

Every nation now needs an effective trading system, but especially so that small and poor. They have it. Everyone will also gain from the huge package of market access results even if they did not get every concession they were seeking from trading partners—it is the biggest market access deal ever negotiated.

However, the essence of the Uruguay Round's achievements is that they are dynamic. The new agreements, the new rules and structures it sets up—all mean a commitment to a continuing process of cooperation and reform of which the agreement in December was only the beginning.

Maintaining the liberalizing momentum will call for continuing effort and vigilance by participating countries. But now their energy can be focused through the Round's greatest innovation; the new World Trade Organisation (WTO) in place of the improvised basis on which the GATT has operated for 45 years, trade will now have a permanent forum appropriate to its importance in the world economy.

Technically speaking, the WTO will oversee the implementation of the Round's results, administer all the agreements in goods, services and intellectual property, and manage the unified dispute settlement system. But beyond these administrative functions, it will raise the political profile of trade a profile which has already been lifted greatly by the Uruguay Round. The WTO will have regular instead of occasional—direct Ministerial involvement. It will have a clear mandate to act as a forum for further trade negotiations. Most of all it will complete the transition from a trading system which largely restricted itself to policies at the border to one which also covers most aspects of domestic policy-making affecting international competition in goods and services, as well as investment.

Through the WTO, the Round will change the way the world economy is shaped. But it is not the final victory over protectionism and unilateralism. Any premature rejoicing would have quickly been cut short by the evidence since 15 December that major economic powers are still ready to take the unilateral approach to trade problems. Arguments for protectionism based on the alleged threat of low-cost competition to production and jobs will not just fade away because the Round is a success. The seductive appeal of "beggar-thy-neighbour" policies is highlighted by the seemingly greater vigour of the lobbies for protectionism than the advocates of open markets.

These dangers—and the speed with which they have resurfaced—make the achievement of the Uruguay Round all the more important, and its successful implementation all the more urgent. Implementation requires more than mutual backslapping about what we have achieved. It requires now that the US, EU and Japan, in particular, rapidly obtain final authority to ratify and also take a lead in providing the WTO with the means to fulfill its mandate.

The success of the Round has come at a time when it is even more vitally needed than anyone could have guessed when it was launched in 1986. Old structures and alignments have been turned inside out in trade as in every other area of international relations. We face a world of change and challenge, in which the reinforced trading system will be a primary source of stability and security.

The developing countries including India have become enthusiastic supporters of the multilateral trading system and the Uruguay Round every if all their demands were not met by industrial countries. The reasons lie in the changing economic policies of many developing countries and the clearer appreciation of the value of the GATT system that has grown along with these changes.

The challenge of new issues in world trade will be a major one for the WTO. The new organisation has to consider issues such as the links between trade and the environment, international competition policy, trade and investment, and trade and labour standards. To say a few words about trade and the environment since it is one area in which GATT member countries have committed themselves already to a comprehensive new work programme. They decided on 15 December, in conjunction with the adoption of the results of the Uruguay Round negotiations, to draw up a work programme on trade and environment by the Ministerial meeting in Marrakesh. Environmental policy-making is one of the most rapidly evolving areas of national and international policy-making, and it is entirely appropriate that emphasis should be placed now in GATT/WTO on ensuring better policy coordination and multilateral cooperation over the linkages between trade and environment.

Permanent Negotiations

The Uruguay Round may well be the last of its kind, but this in no way means the end of multilateral trade negotiations. On the contrary, it means they become a permanent event. Ad hoc negotiating rounds were necessary mainly because the GATT lacked the mandate or the institutional basis to operate the multilateral system to the full on a continuous basis. Between rounds the GATT has tended to lose momentum, often at the very times when it was essential to make the most of the liberalising impulse. This has allowed protectionism and unilateralism to recover and regroup and meant that each round has to start by regaining lost ground.

The positive results of the Uruguay Round will redefine much more than assumptions about trade. If they are exploited with the same determination, courage and commitment that went into concluding the Round, they should mean nothing less than a new start for sustainable growth and a new system of collective economic security for the world.

But if the trading system is now up to the job of supporting multilateral cooperation on such a wide scale, do the other structures of economic cooperation still meet the bill? The establishment of the WTO will put trade and investment on a par—perhaps rather in advance—of cooperation in monetary and financial areas. The WTO will stand alongside its original Bretton Woods sisters, the IMF and the World Bank. The three institutions must learn to work together even more effectively and closely. For example, rather than each body conducting separate reviews of country policies, is there not a case to be made for a more integrated approach on country reviews? But that does not, on its own, add up to effective multilateral economic cooperation. The question really has to be asked seriously: are the G7, the OECD, the regional groupings adequate to provide that cooperation?

It is the next challenge of international economic leadership—the challenge of translating the common interest in global growth into a practical and effective mechanism for solving our common economic problems together. So, the Ministers meeting in Marrakesh is an historic event which will establish the World Trade Organisation and put in place the new multilateral trading system, they will be making not an end, but a beginning.

4

International Trade with the Consumer's Money

When trade polices are discussed nationally or internationally people as consumers are largely forgotten. Despite their numbers, they do not carry the weight that producers and other lobbies command. Individually, consumers are seldom informed about how the availability, quality, price and choice of the hundreds of items which they buy in the shops each year are affected by trade policy decisions. If they know how much of their household budgets are determined by decisions to protect individual industries and for how little effect they might be shocked.

Equally, when it is debated publicly, the benefits that would fall to the consumer are usually ignored. This brief study is an attempt to put the consumer interest squarely in the public arena.

How do Government Decisions on Trade Affect the Consumer?

Virtually all-protective policies mean higher prices for the consumer. And if it is not a consumer who pays, it will be domestic producer. These are some of the main actions taken by national authorities.

Government frequently and for the most part, legally raise revenue and protect domestic industries by imposing duties on imported products. If a product has a 25 per cent tariff, the price in the shop will normally be 25 per cent more than its price at the port or airport.

Global quotas and other numerical limits on imports are sometimes legal sometimes not. Either way the intention is to restrict access to the market in such a away that domestic producers of the same product can raise their prices without being forced out of business through lack of competitiveness. Quotas are frequently preferred by those demanding protection because the impact on prices is less obvious than with a tariff. Once again, prices go up in the shops and limits may be so narrow that goods disappear form the shelves altogether.

Voluntary export restraints are quotas of an even more costly kind for the importing country. They allow foreign suppliers to charge higher prices than would be possible under a tariff or normal quota. By "bribing" the exporter this way, opposition to the protection is reduced.

Subsidies are sometimes paid to domestic producers to help them compete with import competition by keeping their costs artificially low. This keeps prices down. Unfortunately, the consumer as a taxpayer ends up paying for the subsidy. In so doing, he is prevented from keeping more of his income to spend on other goods, which may be produced by more efficient industries. One thing is sure once industries get used to subsidies, it is very hard to wean then away.

Rules permit governments to impose extra duties on imports where products are shown to be dumped (sold below the normal price in the exporting country) or subsidised, and where the effect of dumping or subsidisation is demonstrated to damage the corresponding domestic industry. While these duties may be justified, they nevertheless always serve to raise the price for consumers to knock products completely out of the market. Yet very few, if any, countries give much weight to consumer interest when deciding whether to impose such penalty duties. And their use has grown disturbingly in recent years.

Governments usually impose standards of safety, quality, public health and environmental protection for good reasons often in the interests of consumers. Sometimes, however, the standards and the procedures, which enforce them, are no more than hidden protections for domestic producers. In imposing unnecessary measures on imports, governments penalize consumers through higher prices and the non-availability of goods.

Protection tends to be loaded towards the products, which are essentials for any family. Consequently, since the essentials command the biggest proportion of the household budgets of poor families, protection acts as a regressive tax.

Clothing is a good example. The multifibre arrangement acts on low-cost products, raising prices and restricting availability, meanwhile up-market goods are seldom affected. Moreover, for the poor consumer, the effect is further exaggerated. Foreign producers will tend to export higher quality end, therefore, more expensive goods, in order to maximize their profits from the quota. This quality upgrading effect not only reduces disproportionately the supply of lower-priced clothing, but may also affect the supply of children's clothing.

Consumers have enjoyed an enormous growth in the range and quality of products in their shops as a result of the multilateral training system. Many fruits and vegetables are available even out of season throughout the year. Exotic foods, never seen just ten or twenty years ago, are now commonly found on supermarket selves. Cut flowers are being transported fresh by cargo plane daily from one country to the other. The range and sophistication of domestic electronic products would have been unimaginable had their development not been spurred by the availability of a global market.

Household Costs are not the Consumer Cost which go up

Many industries are also consumers of imported goods. Manufacturers can depend on cheaper and better products from overseas in order to maintain their own competitiveness in their domestic market and, especially, in their export markets.

The best example is Steel. Many companies require either specialty steel or basic steel products at the lowest possible prices. Unfortunately, because of export restraints, formal quotas, anti-dumping and countervailing duties and high tariffs.

Sometimes they cannot even find the precise type or quality of steel they need. They are, therefore, put at a huge competitive disadvantage.

Semi-conductors and other electronic components are also subject to this self defeating form of protection. Just as the price of steel puts up the price of automobiles, so high tariffs, anti-dumping duties and quotas on electronic components puts up the prices of video recorders, personal computers and other advanced consumer electronic products. Meanwhile foreign competitors continue to buy their semi-conductor inputs at world market prices.

But is One of the Prices a Lowering of Public Health and Safety Standard?

It has been suggested that some measures to ensure safe goods for consumer and to prevent the spread of pests of diseases among animals and plants do not amount to unjustified barriers to trade.

The first point is that if there is some justification for them, these measure—even if they restrict trade—are completely permissible. The main objective is to make them transparent, to discourage arbitrary decision-making and discrimination and to minimize any restriction on trade.

The second point is that would encourage government to establish measures consistent with international standards and guidelines. This is important because it could mean a general raising of standards: in many areas even advanced industrial countries do not meet international standards on food safety.

Third, the government has to impose more stringent standards than those agreed internationally. The only condition is that a government so doing might, if challenged, be required to show scientific evidence or some kind of risk assessment to support the measure.

It should also be noted that with the reduction of agricultural subsidies which encourage unlimited production (those supporting farmers' income directly will still be permitted) consumers should see more products produced by less chemical intensive farming methods in the shops.

5

Revisiting Bretton Woods

Reforming the World Trade and Finance System

That leading trio of major multilateral economic institutions (the International Monetary Fund and World Bank in Washington D.C. and the WTO in Geneva) were created from the ashes of World War Two to build a strong, coordinated, international set of economic arrangements. They did well. Their contributions significantly forges systems of cooperation between governments which, in turn, encouraged global economic growth and development.

But, is it time now to revisit Bretton Woods, that location in the hills of New Hampshire, where half a century ago U.S. Treasury Secretary Harry Dexter White, British economist Lord Keynes, and many others, set the plans for the post-war multilateral economic system?

The question is not academic. It was being asked recently in an unprecedented scale in the annual meeting of the IMF and World Bank in Washington D.C. The questioning came for three critical reasons:

First, there is a widespread view that a strong supranational institution is urgently required in the currency arena. The IMF has been absorbed with medium-term economics assistance programmes and appears to be attaching low priority to its original purpose: the IMF's Articles of Agreement declare the Fund's purpose is: "To promote international monetary cooperation through a permanent institution which provides the machinery for consultation and collaboration on international monetary problems".

Second, the WTO has brought tempers to the boil in many developing countries and created fears. The WTOs failure is serving now as stimulus for the growth of regional trade blocs, based upon major industrial countries and open to relatively few developing countries.

Third, the World Bank has taken a backseat when it has come to advancing Western support for the poorest nations. There was a times when the President of the World Bank would use his office to rally international opinion and publicly urge the industrial nations to take a more constructive and more generous approach to the developing nations. In recent times the leadership of the institution has been silent. It has become mired in administrative matters, willing to bow to IMF leadership and content to seek to influence development thinking through the publication of economic research reports.

World Bank Subordinate to IMF

At the same time, the World Bank has come to play second fiddle to the IMF. The Fund has engineered itself into a position a leadership in economic policy discussion with developing countries and with the former command economies of East Europe and Central Asia. The World Bank does not provide programme lending of any kind until a borrowing country first has an IMF programme in place While the two institutions are totally distinct in legal and financial terms, the Bank has accepted a subordinate position to the IMF.

These three phenomena are not encouraging for the health of global economy and from the perspective, in particular, of the developing countries.

On the monetary front there is a need to protect the interests of developing and emerging countries from the vagaries of the super-economic powers. Most of the governments of the world have looked on hopelessly as Japan, Germany and the United States, have pursued nationalist economic policies that have played havoc with the currency system. Most of the world's trade is booked in the currencies of these countries and when those currencies spin out of control, so concluding trade deals and securing investment agreements becomes far more complex.

Uncertainty and instability in the world's currency systems are menaces that the IMF was expressly designed to counter. But the IMF has become so engaged in development lending (it now talks of providing programmes to some 80 countries) that its need for financial resources of its own is growing rapidly. That need makes it difficult for the Fund to be critical of its most powerful members. It cannot bite the hands that feed it. Thus, calls to the major nations for fiscal restraint, monetary discipline and international cooperation are made in muted tones.

The Fund, however, must respond to the mounting recognition that some supranational mechanisms are needed to survey the international economic landscape, to ring the alarm bells, to push and shove for meaningful consultation and to place blame on those whose policies are so nationalistic that they endanger the international system. IMF surveillance of the major economic power needs teeth.

The Fund should concentrate once again on using its influence and its expert staff to enhance international understanding of the complexities of the global trading and financial system. By this means it can rebuild its influence with the major powers. While it is unrealistic at this juncture to call for the IMF to become the world's central bank, it could serve as a vitally important convener of consultative processes designed to attain the objectives that its founders decreed: "To facilitate the expansion and balanced growth of international trade, and to contribute thereby to the promotion and maintenance of high levels of employment and real income and to the development of the productive resources of all members as primary objectives of economic policy".

The IMF's role should be enhanced. It should blend its monetary miles with new trade roles. The WTO been the forum for negotiations and for the supervisions of agreements. WTO does not undertake projects, it does not have powers to influence the policies of its most powerful members and it does not have the prestige needed to provide real leadership. It is time the WTO was merged into the IMF.

Trade and Finance Belong Together

It makes little sense to split issues of international capital flows from trade questions. The globalisation of trade and investment has brought these disciplines close together. If forging satisfactory agreements is often difficult, then this in part is due to the fact that distinct organisations have leadership for distinct parts (WTO for trade and IMF for money) and there is no effective mechanism for cooperation. It is also the case that within national governments the trade and finance ministries are often in conflict and face insufficient pressure to coordinate. If the IMF managed both trade and monetary negotiations on the global scale, then this would add pressures on trade and finance ministers to work together.

Returning to its original monetary roles and adding a major trade role should be more than enough to keep the IMF busy. It would be logical, particularly in such circumstances, that the Fund return to the World Bank the development financing roles that it has assumed in recent years and that diverted it from its original purposes.

The IMF's Articles stress that one of its purposes is "to give confidence to members by making the general resources of the Fund temporarily available to them under adequate safeguards, thus providing them with opportunity to correct maladjustment in their balance of payments without resorting to measures destructive of national or international prosperity".

The Fund might argue that the World Bank should confine itself to infrastructure and social project finance and technical assistance and leave all programme lending to the IMF. The reality is that the World Bank discovered to an increasing degree, starting with experiences with Turkey in 1979 and then with many highly indebted nations from 1982 onwards, that the best development projects will fail in countries where wholly unsatisfactory economic policies are in place. The Bank has also recognized the pain and complexity of adjustment and that countries embarking on adjustment policies enter upon a multi-year process: a process better geared to types of financing arrangements that the World Bank can offer, than those provided by the IMF.

Avoid Duplication of Effort Between IMF and World Bank

The experiences of the last decade have strengthened the World Bank's understanding of macro-economic policy reform and enhanced its capacity to provide comprehensive policy from support to its member countries. Cooperation with the IMF has improved, but it is also second best option and an expensive one. There remains too much duplication between the Fund and the Bank. The biggest cost is paid by the borrowing countries—ministers and their immediate subordinates spend endless hours negotiating separately with IMF and World Bank teams and developing duplicative reports.

Reform is only necessary when things are not working well. Today there is enormous scope for improvement in the global trading, monetary and development areas. The three prime institutions created for these areas are not performing well enough. Reform is urgent: the WTO should be merged with the IMF, the IMF should refocus on issues fundamental to securing a healthy global monetary (and trading) system and withdraw form the aid game: and the World Bank should have enlarged scope and provide more leadership on the development front.

Such reforms will not end the problems that our world economic system faces and their significance will be largely determined by the support they receive from the leaders of the most powerful industrial nations, irrespective of the zeal of the officials within the IMF and World Bank. Today, in the midst of prolonged international slump where nobody is satisfied with the ways in which the international system is operating, there is an important opportunity to secure backing in the capitals of the world's super-economic power for the types of reform that are articulated here.

6

High World Trade Growth Vs. Output:

WTO see Link to Globalisation

World trade in merchandise goods is expected to increase in volume by 8 per cent in 1995 down marginally on the very high 9½ per cent for 1994. Although the current outlook is for a further modest slowing next year, trade growth will remain above the average of the past decade.

Recent trade growth figures continue to exceed world production growth by a large margin in 1995 probably by a factor of almost three and next year close to double. This persistent pattern relates closely to the "globalisation" of the world economy; a process which, brings far-reaching benefits and which can be promoted through the further development of the multilateral trading system.

The recent growth is as follows:

- a 13 per cent rise pushed the value of world merchandise trade past the $4,000 billion mark for the first time, to $4,090 billion;
- an 8 per cent increase in the value of trade in commercial services, to $1,100 billion, after near stagnation in 1993;
- a 23 per cent increase in the dollar value of merchandise trade in the first six months of 1995 which, allowing for the depreciation of the US dollar,

is consistent with a full-year growth in trade volume of 8 per cent.

Globalisation

Over the period from 1950 (when the process of trade libealisation through the early GATT Round got under-way) to 1994, the volume of world merchandise trade increased at an annual rate of slightly more than 6 per cent and world output by close to 4 per cent. Thus, during those 45 years world merchandise trade multiplied 14 times and output 5½ times. However, the excess of trade growth over output growth varied; from an average of a mere half percentage point in the period 1974-84 to nearly 3½ percentage points in the most recent 10 years. In fact, the excess during the years since 1990 has been much higher still but it is not yet clear whether or not this represents a permanent shift to a faster rate of increase in the world's trade-to-output ratio.

To the question "will globalisation continue?" In this regard one has to observe two factors—technological change and the evolving strategies of firms and individual investors—impart a natural momentum to global integration. It is government policies which can speed-up, slow down or even reverse progress on global integration. In this context, the role of non-discrimination—in particular, through the "most-favoured-nation" (MFN) clause—is examined.

The MFN Clause

MFN was the centrepiece of a multiplicity of bilateral trade agreements reached in Europe in the second half of the 19th century, a period marked by very low tariffs and rapidly increasing trade. In contrast, the 1920s and the 1930s saw effects to restore liberal trade through international trade conferences rather than legally-binding commercial treaties based on MFN. The failure of these efforts contributed to the Great Depression and provided some of the roots of military confrontation in 1939. It was only after the War that negotiations established what became the GATT, a multilateral contract consisting of rules and disciplines and based firmly (Article) on MFN treatment.

The GATT system has been a post-war bulwark against a return to the trade chaos of the 1930's. In the 1990's, a disintegration of the globalised international economy on the scale of 1930's is almost unthinkable. In contrast, today "the threat that would be posed by a loss of credibility of the multilateral rules" (now represented by the WTO) would be "a fracturing of the global economy into inward-looking and potentially antagonistic trading blocks".

One can suggest two safeguards against such an eventuality:

- the examination of new ways to ensure that free-trade areas and customs unions remain outward-looking and complement rather than compete with the multilateral trading system; and
- progress in dealing, at the multilateral level, with new issues tied directly to the further evolution of the global economy. These include telecommunications, financial services, environment, competition and investment policies among others.

Progress in dealing with these and other issues at the multilateral level will have a significant impact on the future pace of global integration, both directly and through its impact on the credibility of the multilateral system in influencing the broad spectrum of national trade policies.

7

Free Trade as Peacemaker:

The Benefits of an Open World Trading System

Globalisation by free trade according to the principles of the World Trade Organisation (WTO) offers the only realistic opportunity to integrate the world peacefully and in time to prevent a major disaster. The primacy of the economy over politics is the most important vehicle for a successful world domestic policy.

Since Adam Smith, traditional economic theory has on principle been well-disposed towards free trade. Free trade enables better use of the world's economic resources than does national protectionism. Countries can concentrate on their respective strength and draw from their trade partners the goods they need, but do not produce. But there have always been objections against free trade.

The international trade system has always been encumbered by disparate accusations of unfair competition. The fear that foreign competitors use unfair methods, such as dumping, as and is widespread. If one were to believe all the charges of dumping that are made, then international trade would have been completely destroyed long ago. Great restraint should be exercised with respect to allegations of dumping if one is interested in maintaining an interweaving of international economic activities.

The Free Trade Oppsition Cloaks itself in Dumping Charges

The modern form of the struggle against free trade cloaks itself in the accusation of ecological dumping or social dumping.

With this difficult subject matter, one should not make sweeping generalisations. These things also are not gone into in detail in what follows.

Environmental protection is an asset that every economy produces at the cost of other assets. The people's preferences for the asset of environmental protection probably varies from country to country. It is also completely legitimate and does not at all distort trade if the environmental provisions-in line with the different national preferences—vary from country to country.

In the rich western European economic region, one should guard against a new form of cultural imperialism. It is not for this part of the world to impose its preferences for environmental assets on other countries, especially Third World countries. Free world trade brings not only economic advantages. Even more important is its contribution to lasting world peace.

In view of world population growth, every standstill in the movement towards a peaceful world society must be seen as a step backwards. We are compelled to run a race between the growing problems and the development of stable institutions to overcome them peacefully at global level. Economic history since the end of the Second World War shows clearly that free trade under the old GATT was of decisive importance for the prosperity of the industrialised nations.

The principle of help for self-help has nowhere been applied so consistently as on the free world market. In reverse, the examples of countries that cut themselves off from the world market show the disastrous consequences of the rigidity of a society which shuns the pressure of international competition.

Revolutionary Success of Open-Market Policies

The West's policy of open markets pursued since 1948 and reinforced since 1989 has led to a dynamism which, in the true meaning of the word, is revolutionary. More than half the word population now lives in countries with annual GDP growth rates of more than 5 per cent. Europe is not among that group, which may be why it also stands somewhat apart in its mentality.

Certainly, there also can be undesirable trends in free trade. There is not ideal systems; one must choose between imperfect potentialities. However, no realistically better substitute for the free trade system is in sight, not even with respect to the goals of a pacified world: an ecological sound world economy and a balance of global dimensions between the poor and the rich. An ideal government of philosopher kings armed with absolute power certainly could do some thing better than does free trade—but such a government remains fictitious. There are tangible and narrow limits to what the political system, whether democratic or not, can effect in a positive sense. This is how the structural conservatism of democratic and other political systems impedes the timely assertion of reforms necessary to achieve a world peace society.

The GATT was turned into the World Trade Organisation (WTO) a few years ago. Besides extending the free trade principle to services and additional agricultural sectors the new agreement foresees above all the full inclusion of the Third World in the system. The agreement commits the industrialised nations to open their markets to developing and threshold countries.

Other important points are the strengthening and tightening of the dispute mediation process. Based on a system of relatively independent ad hoc panels, it permits complaints against WTO member countries for violations of the agreement. Thus, what is arising here is an effective global jurisdiction within the meaning of a peaceful world domestic policy.

Exclusion as Penalty

The decisive sanction mechanism of the WTO—which is not a specialist organisation of the United nations—is the threat of exclusion. Exclusion would deny the penalised country free access to the markets of WTO members on the basis of most favoured nation status. This is a threat that requires no armed force, but is very effective. No country can still afford to do without the beneficial effects on prosperity that participation in international trade brings.

Thus, with the threat of denial of access to world markets for violating WTO rules, and the guarantee of a more or less fair competition for a country's own products for abiding by them, a non-military sanctions system has come into being. That is substantial progress on the path to a pacified world.

Certainly, this sanction system's sphere of influence is limited for the time being. Essentially, it will be used to assert the game rules of free trade. It offers no legal grounds for pressing other goals, such as on human rights. Attempting to expand it in this direction would for the foreseeable future put the entire system at risk.

In the current debate on globalisation, the question arises of whether the world economic institutions should not be converted in this manner, that politics regains its autonomy, and that the primacy of politics can be restored. The critics of globalisation point to the constraints to adjust which the world economy exercises on national or continental politics. However well this demand for the primacy of politics may be justified in philosophical terms, it virtually comes down to a demand for the ascendancy of the conservative principle.

Danger of a Slowed-Down World Integration

The demand for the primacy of politics is gaining strength from the desire to avoid the pressure to adjust which the dynamics of world events are exerting. It is today a conservative, and in fact a reactionary, longing for the (Utopian) return of the functioning European welfare state of two or three decades ago. If it were asserted, it would mean practically slowing down world integration. It would run dead against the goal of a world policy based on a desire for peace.

The present primacy of the economy over politics—in terms of the free movement of goods, services and capital—is basically nothing more than the priority of the global principle over the provincial, the national principle. As such, it gives the principle of change pre-eminence over the principle of maintaining the status quo. What gives the primacy of the economy its legitimacy? Probably not the thought that world peace and better be secured by this means. Its legitimation lies in the very indirect economic success that the free trade system delivers. For the reflective observer, the question remains of whether this legitimation is sufficient.

To answer this question, however, and particularly if one pleads for maintaining the ascendancy of the economy, it appears appropriate to outline the consequences that can be expected from further integration of the world economy. As can be seen today in East and Southeast Asia, the growth dynamics of the world economy will lead to a marked rise in the living standards of a large part of the Third World.

Do Not Exclude Poor Countries from the Competition

The global consequences of Asia's growth should not have been seen only negatively. While it also may mean, for example, a great burden on the global climate, it leads at the same time to an acceleration of the process of falling birth rates and thus to an earlier stabilisation of the world population. Prosperity for the third Wrld is so far the only realistic answer to the urgent problem of population growth. And free competition on the world market in the only reliable means of achieving this prosperity in the course of some decades.

Despite ecological sacrifice in the medium term, continuation of Third World growth is the only way to solve the long-term ecological problems. One also should not forget that only those who can eat their fill and have a roof over their heads are prepared to reflect on ecology and discuss it.

As for the rest, the balance between rich and poor is more acceptable when the poor become richer than when the rich become poorer. That applies also at the international level. The market and access to it are peaceful sanctions of the world economic system on the basis of free trade. Those who are hungry and have nothing more to lose are more of a danger to world peace than those who have eaten their fill. The ruse of covering up domestic problems by cross border military aggression will become less attractive to the degree that a country's own economy is integrated in the global economic system. The more countries are economically dependent on each other, the more unlikely it is that they will wage war on each other.

Globalisation by free trade according to the principles of the WTO offers the only realistic opportunity to integrate the world peacefully and in time to prevent a major disaster. The primacy of the economy is the most important vehicle for a successful world domestic policy.

8

Add Value, Go Global:

Can Southern Firms Break into Export Markets?

The global economy has changed beyond recognition over the last decade. Widespread economic policy reform and in particular trade liberalisation have open up new opportunities for developing countries. In poor countries, however, the consequences of trade liberalisation are not always positive. What can the private sector do to respond better and make the most of new trading opportunities? What factors have limited the impact of economic reforms on export performance?

Why have exports from poorer countries failed to increase more rapidly following trade liberalisation? What can be done to improve performance? Research on the response of firms in the private sector to economic reform can underpin new approaches to export promotion for poorer developing countries. For a long time, protective trade policies, poorly performing state-owned industries and state controls over the private sector were blamed for poor export performance in Africa and South Asia. Now that some of these problems have been remedied, other obstacles have come to light.

The effect of economic liberalisation and adjustment on the performance of poor countries has been cause for concern. Trade liberalisation should increase incentives to export and facilitate business enterprise by encouraging private ownership through privatisation and by attracting foreign investment. Macroeconomic stability ought to boost business confidence and performance. All these factors should promote exports, offsetting job and income losses caused by the closure or reorganisation of inefficient enterprises and industries yet, although some degree of reform and stability it is without export growth that was expected.

Trade reform and macroeconomic stability may be necessary conditions for improved export performance put by them are insufficient. The obstacles to improving export performance are numerous and there is no easy policy answer. The research programme examined export performance at three levels.

- Regional: how trade strategies should vary with skills and natural resource endowments
- National: factors influencing the export performance of manufacturing
- Sectoral: the performance of particular sectors of the economy.

The East Asian economies have shown that developing countries can complete successfully in global markets. For many, they provide a blueprint for economic growth applicable to many poor countries

South Asia's comparative advantage lies in its abundant unskilled labour, while Africa's lies in its abundant natural resources. Different export promotion strategies are essential. South Asia's best prospectus are in labour-intensive manufacturing: the region's low level of exports would soar over the next decade if current obstacles to trade were reduced. Africa's exports could also increase but its biggest potential in primary products that need little educated labour and abundant natural resources.

Some African countries could also be substantial exporters of manufacturers, but their actual manufactured exports in most cases now fall far short. Comparing Ghana to Mauritius—one of Africa's most successful exporters of manufactured goods differences in firm-level efficiency are apparent Mauritian firms have more capital per worker and use it more efficiently.

Reducing trade barriers is not sufficient. Wages in Ghana would have to be substantially lower to offset low labour productivity. Alternatively, labour productivity will have to be drastically improved if Ghanian firms are to compete successfully in export markets with wages at current levels.

Even when companies use capital and labour efficiently, poor infrastructure is a frequent stumbling products to export markets—an acute problem in landlocked countries and equally acute for manufacturers as research on Uganda clearly shows. What huts manufacturing exporters is being hit by the high cost of transporting their output to foreign markets and of transporting the materials they need from abroad. The cost penalties resulting from geography and poor infrastructure are far greater in Uganda than from high tariffs and other import restrictions.

Southern firms can still break into export markets, however, developing—country firms do export to markets with exacting standards for product quality, reliability of delivery, and consumer safety. Two crucial aspects, however, are often overlooked:

- Non-manufacturing sectors, such as tourism and horticulture, generate significant employment and offer opportunities for supplying increasingly sophisticated products. Although manufacturing is considered more attractive, certain areas of tourism and horticulture can be equally appealing.
- New export opportunities are created as southern producers establish closer links with foreign customers. Producers of labour-intensive products such as garments, horticulture and footwear frequently depend on large retailers and specialist international traders for designs, information about demand and technical support.

Supermarkets make key decisions about which fruits and vegetables to grow, how they should be produced and processed and which firms should be included in the business. Strategic decisions by international producers and retailers in the footwear industry have been crucial in developing new production locations such as Vietnam and Romania. Similarly, work on automotive components production in South Africa and India illustrates how global sourcing by the leading motor companies closes off some markets and opens up others. Export prospects can only be evaluated in the light of global restructuring in these industries.

Emphasising global linkages does not mean that developing countries are powerless in the face of global forces. Even in tightly-structured industries, there is scope for national policy and national strategy. Further more, there are important export sectors that are not structured in this way. Some tourism is dominated by large northern firms and is heavily import-dependent, but there is also enormous potential and national policy will be crucial in shaping the industry and its contribution to the economy as a whole.

For southern firms to break into export markets, certain issues must be addressed, especially in Africa. Some are recognised as important policy issues—investing in human capital and improving infrastructure for example. As one set of constraints are reduced—such as removing policy—induced distortions through trade liberalisation—another set takes precedence. In response to the integration of global markets, southern producers must join the global distribution chains to ensure markets for their exports.

These findings impose hard choice on developing countries. Should a firm allocate limited funds for investment in human capital or investment infrastructure? Future research might contribute by quantifying relative rates of return. On another level, countries may worry about the independence and autonomy of local producers if they are to join a global chain typically donated by northern companies. Rules regulate governmental trade and investment policies but who controls the global buyers and multinatinal companies whose decisions have such huge impacts on developing countries?

9

Trading Towards Peace

The reason why trade has such a vital part to play in building peace is because it means lowering barriers—not only to goods and services but among nations and peoples. The elimination of barriers creates interdependence and interdependence creates solidarity. The history of the last fifty years has shown us all the undeniable benefits of lowering trade barriers and opening economies.

Clearly every region has its own characteristics, and it would be wrong to imagine that the same blueprint can apply everywhere and in the same way. Any region which was for thousands of years at the crossroads of world trade should regain its place in the centre, because doing so will help build peace as well as prosperity. This is why the numerous applications for accession to the WTO from various countries are so significant. The first is through regionalism. There are several efforts at regional trade and economic initiatives among countries, and that such initiatives will be encouraged to reduce positive results. Regional initiatives are important because they can help countries at a comparable level of development to move relatively quickly in opening their economies and in deepening their interdependence.

However, the rapid advance of global economic integration means that while regional initiatives remain important, they are not sufficient by themselves to address successfully the new perspectives of the international economy. That is why there is a need for second track, which is the rule-based multilateral system. And that is why the multilateral system is of fundamental importance to the economic prosperity of any region.

As the first major international institution to be created in the post-Cold War era, the WTO offers a promise of the kind of global economic architecture which need in the coming decades. Its culture is firmly rooted in the tradition of consensus-building and cooperation among sovereign countries. And the WTO embodies rights and obligations negotiated by consensus, approved and ratified by each government and each Parliament, and they are enforceable, not through the crude exercise of economic power, but through the rule of law. The alternative would be a power-based system—who would want to chose this option ?

But most importantly, the WTO is an organisation which brings all countries—from all corners of the world and from all levels of development—together as equals. There is no weighted voting, no exclusive clubs, no inner and outer circles. Developing countries representing 80% of constituency sit as equals with industrialised countries to write the rules of a shared trading system.

This new unity of developing and developed countries inside a single system will be credited as the greatest achievement of the multilateral system. But this unity is still fragile: We cannot allow it to be broken: This is why, in preparing the agenda of the first Ministerial meeting in Singapore, have recognised the particular difficult task facing developing countries in implementing the Uruguay Round commitments. They have also acknowledged the challenges they face in contemplating the necessary work programme.

The integration of developing countries as equal partners in the multilateral system is one of the most important challenges in shaping the economic order of the 21st century. This is a shared responsibility of developed and developing countries alike. There is no rational alternative to this objective. The evolution of the global economy makes that clear.

Now there is a need to work together as equal partners to ensure the full integration, and all other developing and transition economies, into the global economy and the rule-based multilateral trading system. In conjunction with this there is a need to encourage, notably the growth of regional economic cooperation. The alternative is a vicious circle where economic isolation feeds greater political instability which in turn leads to greater economic isolation. The road to a lasting peace in the world begins, not ends, with economic integration and interdependence. Taking this message to heart will help build a future where it is goods, services, and investment that cross borders—not missiles and soldiers.

10

The Truth about Global Competition

The Economic Myths behind Globalisation

Local communities everywhere are on the front lines of what might well be characterized as World War III. It is not the nuclear confrontation between East and West—between the Soviet Union and the United States—that we once feared. It is a very different kind of conflict. There is no clash of competing military forces and the struggle is not defined by national borders. But it does involve an often violent struggle for control of physical resources and territory that is destroying lives and communities at every hand. It is a struggle between the forces and institutions of economic globalisation and the communities that are trying to reclaim control of their economic lives. It is a conflict between competing goals—economic growth to maximize profits for absentee owners versus creating healthy communities that are good places for people to live. It is a competition for the control of markets and resources between global corporations and financial markets on the one hand and locally owned businesses serving local markets on the other.

Two things of fundamental importance to each and every one of us is now very much at stake.

- Will people and communities control their local resources and economies and be able to set their own goals and priorities based on their own values and aspiration? Or will these decisions be left to global financial markets and corporations that are blind to all values save one —instant financial returns?

- Will the life sustaining resources produced by the regenerative capacities of our planet's ecosystems be equitably shared to provide fo the material needs of all of us who inhabit this bountiful planet, as well as for our children and their children unto the seventh generation and beyond? Or will we allow a global economic system that is now functioning on auto-pilot beyond conscious human control to consume and destroy the ecosystem and our social fabric in its insatiable quest for money?

Economists, politicians, cooperate spokespersons and the media have for year been touting the benefits of the global economy. They have called on us to support trade agreements such as the North American Free Trade Agreement (NAFTA) and the World Trade Organisation (WTO) to remove the constraints of economic borders and open to everyone the opportunities of growth and prosperity in the global economy. They have promised rich rewards for those workers and communities that become successful global competitors.

Many of the most ardent boosters of economic globalisation met earlier in the year at the annual meeting of the World Economic Forum. This Forum has for years brought together top industialists and political figures from around the world to advance the proposition that removing tariffs and other restrictions on the free international flow of trade and money is a key to creating new economic opportunity and prosperity. It thus caused quite a stir when the Forum publicly announced that economic globalisation is producing disastrous consequences that threaten the political stability of the Western democracies. Their warning bears close examination for being one of the most honest and accurate assessments of the consequences of economic globalisation yet produced by leading advocates of that process. The observation is that:

- Economic globalisation is causing severe economic dislocation and social instability.
- The technological changes of the past few years have eliminated more jobs than they have created.

- The global competition "that is part and parcel of globalisation leads to winner-take—all situations; those who come out on top win big, and the losers lose even bigger."
- Higher profits no longer mean more job security and better wages. "Globalisation tends to delink the fate of the corporation from the fate of its employees."
- Unless serious corrective action is taken soon, the backlash could destabilize the Western democracies.

We don't have to go far to find examples of what they are talking about and why people are getting a bit upset as they wake up to the realities of who is winning in the ruthless competition of the global economy. The disparities between the winners and losers in the global competition are becoming more obscene with each passing day.

We are coming to realize that the extravagant promises of the advocates of the global economy are based on a number of myths that have become so deeply embedded in Western industrial culture that we have grown to accept them without examination.

- The myth that growth in GNP is a valid measure of human well being and progress.
- The myth that free unregulated markets efficiently allocate a society's resources.
- The myth that growth in trade benefits ordinary people.
- The myth that growth in trade benefits ordinary people.
- That if freed from governmental interference will provide a clean environment for all and good jobs for the poor.
- The myth that absentee investors create local prosperity.

The Growth Myth

Our measures of growth are deeply flawed in that they are purely measures of activity in the magnetized economy.

Expanded use of cigarettes and alcohol increases economic output both, as a direct consequence of their consumption and because of the related increase in health care needs. The need to clean up oil spills generates economic activity. Gun sales to minors generate economic activity. A divorce generates both lawyer's fees and the need to buy or rent and outfit a new home increasing real estate brokerage fees and retail sales. It is now well documented that in number of other countries the quality of living of ordinary people has been declining as aggregate economic output increases.

The growth myth has another serious flaw. Since 1950, the world's economic output has increased 5 to 7 times. That growth has already increased the human burden on the planet's regenerative systems—its soils, air, water, fisheries, and forestry systems—beyond what the planet can sustain. Continuing to press for economic growth beyond the planet's sustainable limits does two things. It accelerates the rate of breakdown of the earth's regenerative systems—as we see so dramatically demonstrated in the case of many ocean fisheries, and it intensifies the competition between rich and poor for the resource base that remains.

This is vividly illustrated by many of the development projects in India many funded with loans from the World Bank and other multilateral development banks—that displace the poor so that the lands and waters on which they depend for their livelihood can be converted to uses that generate higher economic returns—meaning converted to use by people who can pay more than those who are displaced.

The Myth of Free Unregulated Markets

It is almost inherent in the nature of markets that their efficient function depends on the presence of a strong government to set a framework of rules for their operation. We know that free markets create monopolies, which government must break up to maintain the conditions of competition on which market function depends.

We also know that markets only allocate efficiently when prices reflect the full and true costs of productions. Yet in the absence of governmental regulation, market incentives persistently push firms to cut corners on safety, pay workers less than a living wages, and dump untreated toxic discharges into a convenient river. In our present competitive context if management does not take such measures, they are likely to be replaced by the owners of brought out by someone with less scruples who will.

The Myth of Free Trade

Many so-called trade agreements, such as the North American Free Trade Agreement (NAFTA) and the World Trade Organisation (WTO) are not really trade agreements at all. They are economic integration agreements intended to guarantee the rights of global corporations to move both goods and investments where ever they wish-free from public interference and accountability. WTO is best described as a bill of rights for global corporation.

The Myth that Economic Globalisation is Inevitable

Many of the people who claim globalisation is a consequence of inevitable historical forces are paid to promote that message by the same global corporation that have invested millions of dollars in advancing the globalisation policy agenda.

The Myth that Corporations are Benevolent Institutions

The corporation is an institutional invention specifically and internationally created to concentrate control over economic resources while shielding those who hold the resulting power from liability for the consequences of its use. The more national economies become integrated into a seamless global economy, the further corporate power extends beyond the reach of any state and the less accountable it becomes to any human interest or institution other than a global financial system that is now best described as a gigantic legal gambling casino.

All over the world people are indeed waking up to the truth about economic globalisation and are taking steps to reclaim and rebuild their local economies. Such communities face basic choices as to how they will divide their efforts between competing for a share of the declining pool or good jobs that global corporations offer and working to create locally owned enterprises that sustainably harvest and process local resources to produce the jobs and the goods and services that local people need to live healthy, happy, and fulfilling lives in balance with the environments.

Our experience with the real consequences of economic globalisation is pointing to many important lessons. One such lesson is that economies should be local, rooting power in the people and communities who realized their well being depends on the health and vitality of their local ecosystem. If it is protetionist to favour local firms and workers who pay local taxes, live by local rules, respect and nurture the local ecosystems, compete fairly in local markets, and contribute to community life—then let us all prouddly proclaim ourselves to be protectionist.

Such choices are not isolationist. To the contrary, they create a foundation for creative cooperation with our neighbours—whether they be in the United States or in other countries—to share experience, ideas, and technology—and to join in international solidarity in rewriting the rules of the global economy to favour local over global businesses, and to encourage cooperative relations among people and communities. It is our consciousness—our ways of thinking and our sense of membership in a larger community—not our economies-that should be global.

Millions of people are also making an important discovery—that life is about living—not consuming. A life of material sufficiency can be filled with social, cultural, intellectual, and spiritual abundance that place no burden on the plantet.

It is time to assume responsibility for creating a new human future of just and sustainable communities freed from the myth that greed, competition, and mind-less consumption are paths to individual and collective fulfilment. It will take millions of people around the world—linked together into a powerful political coalition aimed at radical political and economic reform to win the war that global capital is waging against us.

11

Export Subsidies

A Distortion to Trade in Agriculture

Export subsidies are generally considered one of the most distorting trade tools used by governments to interfere with commerical markets. Export subsidies allow a government to determine the level and direction of trade solely on the basis of government subsidies, lowering world prices and denying sales for other, more competitive exporters. Not only are export subsidies unfair commercial tools, but, by encouraging surplus production, they encourage adverse environmental practices, waste government budgets, and may delay restructuring and reform of domestic industries. Substantial progress toward eliminating export subsidies will be a critical element of the World Trade Organisation (WTO) negotiations scheduled to begin at the end of this year.

The Situation Today

Under the Uruguay Round Agreement, countries agreed to strictly limit the use of export subsidies. First, products that had not benefited from export subsidies in the past were banned from receiving them in the future. Second, where countries had provided export subsidies in the past, their future use was capped and gradually reduced over 6 to 10 years. Developed countries were required to cut their spending on export subsidies by 36 per cent over six years while also reducing subsidised export quantities by at least 21 per cent on a commodity-specific basis.

Developing countries have until 2005 to cut spending by 24 per cent and subsidised quantities by 14 per cent. Third, countries agreed not to create new schemes that serve as disguised subsidies to get around the product-specific limits. Finally, countries recognised that export credit and food aid programmes were different and exempted them from the new budget and quantity limits, although there was agreement to negotiate disciplines on export credit programmes to ensure that they do not undermine WTO commitments.

Today, the European Union (EU) is the primary export subsidiser—accounting for nearly 85 per cent of the world total. Nearly all other countries agreed in the last round of negotiations not to use or to have only limited resource to use export subsidies. EU farmers, responding to domestic prices that are often twice the world price, produce more products than can be consumed in Europe, but at such high prices that they can be sold abroad only with generous subsidies. These subsidies force other competitors out of the market and discourage production in countries with comparative advantage.

If the EU's extravagant domestic subsidies are the root cause of export subsidies, they are also putting serious pressure on the whole EU system. The need to impose budgetary discipline on EU farm programmes (annual cost, about $46 billion) is becoming increasingly evident, even in Europe, and the EU's goal of epanding its membership to new countries is putting pressure on it to bring its farm programmes into line with other countries, which will help reduce its need to rely on export subsidies in the future.

Areas for Resolution

The upcoming negotiations should continue the work begun in the Urguay Round and eliminate existing export subsidies. There is no economic justification for their continued use. By removing subsidized exports, world prices should increase, and farmers, particularly in the EU, will not be artificially encouraged to overproduce products that they cannot grow competitively.

In addition to eliminating export subsidies, countries should examine the rules defining export subsidies to ensure that countries do not resort to other policy tools that might allow governments to distort markets. Specially, WTO members should to look closely at curbing agricultural state trading export monopolies that can exert undue market power or dispose of surplus commodities on a nonmarket basis. A recent WTO victory by the United States and New Zealand over Canada's special-class system of dairy exports shows that the existing rule against circumvention are effective but must be enforced.

Export credit and food aid programmes were addressed in the Uruguay Round agreement in recognition of the fact that those tools could be disguised as subsidies. These policies may again be on the agenda when the WTO negotiations commence next time. It will be important to ensure that the world's needy continue to have access to imported products, even when financial turmoil roils world markets and limits the ability of developing countries to meet their food and fibre needs.

Certain large exporting nations—primarily in the EU have used export taxes as a supply management tool by intervening in the market to restrict exports when domestic stocks are low. These measures can wreak havoc in international markets, exacerbating price swings and reducing the confidence of net-food-importing countries to abandon trade barriers and rely on the international market to provide food security. Similarly, some exporting countries use differential export taxes to discourage exports of basic products (such as grains or oilseeds); they force exporters to process the product domestically (into flour or oil and meal, for example) and export the value added products.

12

Richer or Poorer?

Achievements and Challenges of Ethical Trade

Ethical trade as an approach to supply chain management has mushroomed in recent years. Northern companies are becoming increasingly concerned with the 'ethics' of their operations and risks to reputation and productivity posed by bad employment practices in global supply chains. But can voluntary private sector codes really improve employment conditions in supply chains?

Ethical trade is one dimension of corporate social responsibility, bringing social issues into the mainstream of commercial supply chain management through the use of codes of conduct. It is sometimes confused with fair-trade which addresses terms of trading for smaller producers, and fosters greater responsibility in supply chain relations.

Ethical trade, on the other hand, focuses on workplace issues, requiring that supplier's in particular meet minimum employment, worker welfare and aspects of human rights standards.

Similar management systems are well established for product safety and environmental issues, Here we focus on the social dimensions of ethical trade and its codes of conduct yet the separation of social and environmental standards is increasingly artificial in global sourcing agreements. A plethora of codes are on of fer. The most numerous are in-houses codes such as Nike's 233 company codes counted in 1999 and the figure is rising.

Suppliers have to comply with and pay for multitude of similar but different codes. Harmonising codes or establishing equivalence is on the agenda but has not yet halted the problem of 'code overload'

At a broader level, industry-specific codes have also been developed. The US Apparel Industry Partnership/Fair Labour Agreement adopted by a number of leading US merchandising companies is a good example. Industry standards are not new, as ISO and EMAS environmental management systems show. Building on ISO principles, Social Accountability International (formerly CEPAA) has development SA8000. This is an independent social standard that can be used as an auditable code throughout the private sector.

Ethical trade is partly a response to consumer and campaigning group pressure in globalised economy. Alliances of companies, NGOs, trade. Developing codes of conduct through a multi stakeholder approach is a striking aspect of ethical trade, bringing together companies, NGOs, trade unions and some government departments. An example of this collaborative approach is the Ethical Trading Initiative (ETI) in the UK. The ETI's baseline code of conduct that corporate members from various industries must comply with as a minimum standard is more than just a code, ETI aims to provide a learning environment and sponsors pilot projects in developing countries to test different methods of monitoring and verification.

Codes of conduct need to be assessed in term of content, implantation and impact. A number of professional auditing companies have moved into his area, some accredited to audit specific codes such as FLA or SA8000. Suppliers audited against a specific code undergo an inspection, and where non-compliance is found, have to take remedial action or risk failing the audit.

Social auditing is a complex process, however, and it can be difficult to spot work place abuse, such as sexual harassment or force overtime, Workers have little confidence in a process that appears to be linked with management, and fear that reporting issues could risk their jobs. Advocates of the multi stakeholder approach argue that effective monitoring and verification of codes must involve local NGOs and trade unions in which workers have trust. Participatory social auditing also a means of raising awareness and of facilitating behavioral change, can help reveal serious management problems. But in many developing countries local organisations lack the capacity to participate: developing sustainable local systems of monitoring and verification remains an important challenge.

Do the advantages of multi-stakeholder approaches outweigh immediate constraints? Ethical trade is a largely northern driven process, reflecting Western ethical thinking and priorities, Southern based initiatives, however, are expanding, raising the possibility of local ownership of codes, collaboration poses challenges. Stronger relationships and better understanding are essential between southern and northern workers, producers, trade unions, and NGOs for codes to work globally.

But there is still scepticism as to the extent of the benefits that ethical trade might bring. Will increasing southern capacity to participate, as the ETI has done in its pilot project, help? Will building trust, confidence and dialogue achieve the objectives of ethical trade, north and south? Child labour is often more complex, however, than codes make it appear. Codes need to address the conditions of all workers within the supply chain, including the least visible; partnerships must include all groups to address these limitations.

The role of government is hotly contested. Can a system whose credibility depends on under-resourced civil society actors, often excluding democratically elected representatives, maintain genuine credibility? If the boundaries between private sector and public sector roles are not defined, the list of private sector responsibilities will become unmanageable. Private sector initiatives are not a substitute for more comprehensive national or international development policies.

What are the consequences of codes? Do they encourage downsizing or reinforce from large suppliers where compliance is more easily monitored? There is a risk that the gains of some will be at the expense of others.

Ethical trade has successfully begun forging partnerships to find solutions. While it might be wrong to assume that ethical trade can change the world, handled wisely it could make a world of difference for some. Yet it is not a panacea for development. Issues that remain unchallenged by ethical trade include:

- The exclusion of companies producing for domestic markets—often bigger employers.
- Underlying causes of poverty and social marginalisation.

13

Promotion of Industry and Foreign Investment in Africa

For more than a decade now industrialisation focusing on the promotion of private sector initiative and the encouragement of foreign investment has been given high rank in economic development policy by the authorities in most African countries. Yet, none of these have materialised with any significant impact in most of sub-Saharan Africa. Consequently, an atmosphere of general disappointment and even discouragement with African industrialisation is spreading, increasing some doubts whether adopted policies and programmes are worth-being pursued. This is certainly not a constructive environment and calls for a revision of assumptions, expectations and the means employed, in order to set more realistic and attainable prospects.

After independence, governments usually took a strong stand in regulating the economy and involved themselves in setting up and controlling a great number of state-owned enterprises. Preference was given to large and often capital-intensive enterprises either in production of basic consumer goods for the domestic markets or primary production and processing of export commodities. The role of private industry was relatively neglected or left without clear incentives to operate in the import substitution small and medium sized enterprises (SME) sector. A skeptical, sometimes hostile attitude prevailed towards foreign investment, which was usually controlled and regulated by restrictive concessions and investment laws.

In the early 1980s it had to be recongised that these policies were rather unsuccessful and could hardly be sustained. Growing budget deficits, high foreign debt and reduced flows of foreign credit imposed a revision of previous orientations. Structural adjustment policies were designed and gradually pursued. They basically implied:

- a general reduction of State control of economies;
- liberalisation of internal markets and opening to international competition;
- market adjustment of currency exchange mechanisms;
- deliberate opening to foreign investment;
- privatisation of State-owned enterprises and promotion of private enterprise in general.

Disappointing Results

However, what are the factual results to-date? Basically, all the global performance data show a rather bleak picture for sub-Saharan Africa in recent years, especially in comparison to other developing regions. Real annual GDP growth barely reached 1.5 per cent and growth of manufacturing industry has not significantly improved. Hence the GDP contribution of manufacturing industry remains below 15 per cent in most countries. Sub-Saharan Africa's share of total export volume stagnates and is the lowest of all developing regions. Exports continue to contain mostly primary commodities and only some 10 per cent of manufactured products. Compared with other regions, Africa continues with the lowest rate of private investment (some 8% of GDP in 1995) . Whereas Latin America and East Asia attract together about 80 per cent of net foreign direct investment to developing regions, the African share fluctuates between 1 and 2 per cent.

Constraints and Opportunities

The major constraints for advanced industrialisation in Africa can be briefly recalled.

Restricted Size of Domestic Markets

This is of prime importance for foreign investment which predominantly seeks access and expansion into new markets But also for local investors, it is a serious obstacle as certain technologies and industrial units need a substantial market size to achieve economies of scale. Regional market integration, often advocated as desirable solution, has not made significant progress for various, apparently quite persistent reasons (of which economic nationalism is one—and not only in Africa).

Comparatively High Factor Cost

Besides labour cost and productivity, which are not a decisive advantage in Africa in comparison to other developing regions, the shortage of skilled manpower with industrial experience, as well as infrastructural environment and logistics and generally a lack of integration (inter-sectoral linkage) are restricting factors.

Scarcity of Foreign Exchange

The general shortage of foreign exchange and the exchange rate fluctuations create major obstacles and uncertainties, especially for local market oriented industries which typically depend strongly on imported inputs. This also seriously restricts investment finance which often has to be contracted, and repaid, in foreign currency.

Lack of Financial Resources

Equity capital resources of African entrepreneurs are generally quite limited, and medium to long-term bank loans are constrained by low savings ratios and restrictive conditions of the banking sector.

Limiting Number of Industrial Entrepreneurs

Most entrepreneurs in African countries are found in the artisanal and small industry sector, whereas the small number of potential investors with the financial strength for medium to large enterprise comes from a trading and service background. The latter are usually led by a short-term profit motive and lack to some extent the relevant management experience for industrial enterprise.

Large-scale Enterprises with Investments above Some ECU 5 Million

If we call this category large, this of course is in relation to the context in most African countries: what is "large" there, might well be considered medium or small-sized from an industrialised country stand-point-and that is part of the dilemma. Typically, in this category, one finds mining and mineral exploitation companies, agricultural commodity production and primary processing enterprises, mostly geared towards export markets furthermore, some industries predominantly in food, beverages, textile and construction materials branches producing for local or sometimes regional markets.

The number of enterprises in this range is not more than a few dozens in most countries and only a few new investment opportunities are appearing or could be envisaged. This is rather a domain where many existing companies are State-owned and are seeking privatisation, or where some of the private-owned companies require rehabilitation and restructuring in order to face competitive market conditions.

With some exceptions there is a general tendency of multinational investors to get less involved in standard commodity production; and further processing of primary mineral and agricultural products is maintained closer to the markets in industrialised countries rather than being shifted to primary producing countries. Hence, for the traditional resource-based industries with export orientation, there will be some scope for quantitative expansion, but rather little real prospect for local further processing and linkage with domestic economies.

Large local market-oriented enterprises will continue to be constrained by limited domestic purchasing power, lack of international competitiveness and a serious shortage of foreign exchange, the latter so much more when they require high import contents. There is usually little scope for a multiplication and diversification in this domain, as often one single enterprise unit covers the entire domestic demand (like petroleum refineries, cement factories, cereal mills, breweries, textile mills). If they present some attraction to private, also foreign investment, this still is often conditioned by protection allowing quasimonopolistic market positions.

Small and Medium-sized Enterprises (SMEs)

The great majority of manufacturing enterprises is in this category. It is basically composed of import substitution activities mostly for local consumer goods; some production and processing of local inputs for export (e.g. nontraditional agro products like vegetables and flowers, wood based products, processed fish) and some labour-intensive manufacturing, typically under free-zone status. There are only a few enterprises producing intermediate or investment goods for the local market (like metal and construction material industries).

As recently evidenced in several African countries (e.g. in Ghana, Zimbabwe and Uganda), considerable growth potential exists and some investment can be mobilised for SMEs. Non-traditional exports provide good opportunities, especially as they earn foreign exchange. Free-zone industries have some potential in selected countries, as already known from Mauritius and indicated by more recent trends e.g. in Madagascar and Cape Verde. But the core potential for SMEs remains probably in domestic markets, which involves the challenge for selective import substitution, where it can be efficient, and for the processing of local materials, with appropriate technologies and unit sizes for the basic local demand.

Perspectives for International Cooperation

Many of the leading multilateral and bi-lateral development institution have adopted policies and are providing programmes, mechanisms and resources to assist the development of industry in Africa, to facilitate private foreign investment as well as various forms of enterprise partnership. The World Bank Group has been particularly active in this domain by creating over the last ten years specialised facilities like the Foreign Investment Advisory Service (FIAS), the African Project Development Facility (APDF), the African Management Services company and the Africa Enterprise Fund (AEF) through which the International Finance Corporation provides direct investment funding to medium-sized companies. The European Union put strong emphasis on private enterprise and investment in the fourth Lome Convention and besides institutional assistance towards a better legislative and administrative environment, offers a comprehensive range of financial and technical support to enterprises. The number of projects implemented by the European Commission, especially geared to small-scale industry by way of technical assistance, credit lines and guarantee funds has grown significantly.

Financial resources managed by the EIB, especially risk capital provided from the European Development Fund, were strongly increased and a significant portion has been devoted to investment in the private sector. Some new mechanisms were introduced to make the use of risk capital more flexible and suitable for direct financing of larger projects and indirect financing of SMEs via local credit institutions. The Centre for the Development of Industry (CDI) has been strengthened for its tasks to promote EU-ACP enterprise partnerships and to support the creation or improvement of SMEs. It is noteworthy that CDI can offer its range of practical services directly to individual investors and existing enterprises.

Hence it appears that, although private foreign investors for Africa are scarce, there is no scarcity of external means and mechanisms to assist African enterprise. Yet there is probably a need to better adapt the means to prevailing conditions, to orientate them with clearer priorities towards effective growth potentials and to coordinate them for higher efficiency.

14

Consuming the Future

Now that we are to reach six billion of us, it is a good point to check again on what sort of lifestyles we pursue and what is the environmental impact of those lifestyles. It is curious that we have spent several decades being concerned about the growing numbers of humankind while not giving at least an equal amount of attention to the levels of living we aspire to, and how many natural resources we chew up thereby and how much pollution and waste we cause.

Everybody is a consumer of sorts. True, every fifth person scarcely qualifies for that designation, consuming goods worth less than $1 per day. Conversely, every seventh person qualifies for a designation of super-consumer, with a cash income at least fifty times greater. These latter are the people who, through their carbon dioxide emissions, are disrupting everybody's climate dozens of times more than the average citizen of One Earth. Fair Play, anyone?

Much as the have-nots seek to match the have's, it is plain their efforts will not work out for a long time to come, at best. If every Chinese person were to consume just one additional chicken per year and if the said chicken were to be raised primarily on grain, this would account for as much grain per year as all the grain exports of the number two exporter, Canada. If the Chinese were to raise their per-capita consumption of beef, now only 4 kgs per year, to that of Americans, 45 kg, and if the additional beef were produced largely in feedlots after the manner of the United States, it would account for as much extra grain as the entire US grain harvgest, less than one third of which is exported. Because of its recent climbing up the food chain toward a meat-based diet, China has become one of the world's leading importers of grain. The global grain market today is around 200 million tons per year, and shows scant scope for significant increase.

As a further measure of its ambitions, the Chinese government has designated the auto industry as one of five industry "pillars". Today China has fewer cars than Los Angeles. If per-capita car ownership, together with oil consumption, were to match that of the United States, China would need 80 million barrels of oil per day—by contrast with the world's 1996 oil output of 64 million barrels of oil per day. The surge in carbon dioxide emissions would be unprecedented.

All this notwithstanding, there are already some 250 million newly affluent people in China. They are people with a household income equivalent to perhaps US$20,000, and enough discretionary income to enjoy the perquisites of the good life as perceived by these nouveaux riches. Top of the shopping lists are meat and more meat, followed by cars whether big or small. These are the badges of success: they show you have arrived.

The new consumers in China are matched by at least 200 million in India, and tens of millions in South Korea, Taiwan, Malaysia and Thailand (the recent economic setbacks have not permanently punctured the economic bubblies). Then there are 200 million more in Brazil, Argentina, Venezuela and Mexico, and more again in Hungary and other countries of Eastern Europe, also Turkey. Put them all together and they total about as many as the 800 million long established consumers in the ultra rich countries (the OECD grouping). When the current economic hiccups in Asia are left behind, the ranks of the new consumers can be expected to rise rapidly.

But they cannot hope to become super consumers. Where would all the extra gain come from? How could the global climate tolerate the huge additional pulse of carbon dioxide? There are all kinds of other environmental reasons to suppose that environmental constraints will become all the more constraining. True, technology could help moderate the environmental impact. We could enjoy twice as much material prosperity while using only half as much natural resources and causing half as much pollution and waste. But the new consumers will want to pursue the American dream to the hilt, and it is hard to see that the best technologies could enable huge numbers of affluent aspirants, perhaps two billion people by 2010, enjoying even half the material prosperity of Americans with average household incomes of $40,000.

But is it true "prosperity"—mental and emotional as well as material? Or is the American dream becoming a nightmare with its harried lifestyles and declining leisure time, where the shopping mall is the ultimate Mecca, and the good life is a case of piling up goodies?

In any case, we cannot expect the new consumers to forego their "rightful share" of affluence unless the long-time affluent agree to cut back on their environmental ruinous lifestyles. It is these communities that must offer a strong example, and soonest. Where is the political leader who will espouse the new vision, however much it may be perceived as the ultimate vote loser?

15

The Future of Work

The advent of an 'intangible' economy does not mean the end of work. But it does mean the end of familiar routines and rhythms, of job security, of rigid hierarchies and career planning.

People are worried about the far-reaching transformation of the economy. Are we heading for "the end of work". Yes, we have reached the end of the road. We are no longer creating jobs in industry and automation is sure to reduce their number in the services sector. The quantity of work is thus inexorably bound to decrease.

This thesis may be popular, but it is also mistaken and harmful. History shows that technological innovation has always created jobs on a large scale. In on way is the current trend leading to "the end of work" Just the opposite; the new economy contains huge pools of new jobs which can more than make up for the inevitable loss of traditional jobs.

Dematerialisation—the shift away from material products—is revolutionizing all aspects of work—its nature, its organisation and its relationship with other activities. Its function is no longer just the manufacture of physical objects but the handling of data, images and symbols, The content of jobs is becoming more abstract. Skilled workers need to know a lot more about mathematics than their fathers or grandfathers did. Even milking cows and manufacturing require more and more calculation, evaluation and control.

Financial, Markets that Never Sleep

The organisation as well as the product of wok is also becoming increasingly intangible. The unity of time, space and action which characterized work in the industrial economy has disintegrated. Work is no longer a regular eight-hours-a-day, five-days-a-week routine. New rhythms have appeard-the hectic pace of financial markets which never sleep, the ups-and-downs of life in show business and the uncertainties of "just-in-time" production where components are delivered a few moments before the final product is assembled.

The new jobs are quitting familiar workplaces such as factories, offices and warehouses. Telework is increasing.Europe's teleworkers may number 10 million by the year 2000, up from one million in 1994.

This upheaval of worktime and workspace is going hand in hand with a functional explosion. The range of skills and types of work is expanding all the time. In the United States, the number of job categories has risen from eighty in the 1940s to nearly 800 today. At the same time, trades are dying out faster and faster, especially in information technology where many jobs have a short life of only a few years. Jobs are becoming simultaneously more evanescent and more pervasive, more dissociated and more integrated. On the one hand, fragmentation in time and space seems to be more extensive than it was in the industrial economy. On the other, information technology is strengthening the links between different stages of work and creating an overall fluidity.

Disparities in Productivity

The new forms of work are non-liner. When handling information, knowledge and feelings, there is no direct relationship between the amount of efforts and the final result. This makes for very wide disparities in productivity. In industry, the ratio of the performance of an average worker to that of a good one is no more than one to five. But in immaterial work, an excellent programmer can be a hundred times more productive than an average one.

Non-linear work means non-linear organisation. The notion of a rigid, formal hierarchy based on unchanging criteria no longer makes much sense. All that matters now is technical, scientific or artistic skill and the ability to establish a solid relationship with the customer. Functional hierarchy is replaced by "brainpower"-authority gravitates to those who create and control the new stock of intangible assets: data, brand image, technological know-how and human capital.

The new techniques for managing human resources are individualizing the assessment of performance. Two people doing the same job may have different salaries and different status. Automatic across-the-board pay rises are being dropped and replaced by bonuses linked to results. There are no sinecures in the new business enterprise, either for rank-and-file employees, supervisors or technicians—the suppose beneficiaries of the new knowledge economy.

Business leaders are no longer a protected species. The head of a big American firm is ten times more likely to be sacked for poor performance now than was the case twenty years ago. The notions of loyalty and of indissoluble links between a firm and its employees are losing their meaning.

The changing nature of work has led to a big increase in so-called non-typical jobs, including part-time, temporary and flexi-time work and short-term contracts. Almost all the jobs created in Europe between 1992 and 1996 were part-time. This trend worries many observers who see it as hidden under-employment or disguised unemployment. But they are overly pessimistic. The growth of non-typical jobs is the result of the convergence of several persistent developments.

Where the New Jobs Are

The shrinking number of jobs in traditional sectors of the economy seems to be a general and irreversible trend. In rich countries as a whole, the share of industrial jobs fell from 28 per cent in 1970 to 18 per cent in 1994. Meanwhile, the share of the services sector grew steadily. Four major new sources of jobs can be identified:

Handling Information and Knowledge: Computer services, research and development, teaching and training account for 40 per cent of knowledge workers. These high-intensity knowledge activities comprised 43 per cent of all new jobs created in the United States between 1990 and 1995, but only 28 per cent of total jobs.

Information Technology: Here there is a shortage of personnel. Professional groups are sounding the alarm and calling on governments to help. In the European Union countries, the imbalance between supply and demand is such that half a million jobs are waiting to be filled.

The Health Sector: The growth of high-intensity knowledge services in this field is related to increased life expectancy and the ageing of the population, and the demand for physical and psychological well-being is also steadily increasing. The growth of expenditure on health is persistent and widespread. For the OECD countries as a whole, this spending grew from 3.9 per cent of GDP in 1960 to 7.2 per cent in 1980 and 8.4 per cent in 1992.

The Leisure Economy. This has triggered the expansion of cultural, sporting and leisure services. It ranges from amusement parks and rock concerts to cultural events such as opera and major art exhibitions. The products of the culture industries have become mass consumer items. Never before have people read so much, listened to so much classical music or visited so many museums. Information Technology is also going to add to this vast range of consumer choice. In sourthern California and New York, the entertainment and multimedia professions are among the main sources of new jobs.

In the labour market, the increase in non-typical jobs is one of the ways in which employers are responding to the pressures of competition and adapting to a global economy which functions seven days a week, twenty-four hours a day. To cope with the new situation, firms are having to figure out how they can use their workers more efficiently and flexibly.

The growth of non-traditional jobs is also due to changing demand. Consumers want to be able to buy a very wide range of goods and services at the drop of hat, or amuse themselves any time, anywhere. To meet this demand, shops and places of entertainment have to be open late at night and on Sundays. Technology encourages this trend: the virtual economy of the Internet never sleeps.

The widening range of types of work also reflects long-term demographic trends, especially the greater number of women workers and longer life expectancy. Some see non-typical jobs as a necessary evil, while others, especially women with children, welcome the change.

The divide between traditional kinds of work and the new jobs is no longer watertight. People are increasingly switching back and forth between the two categories. In the course of a lifetime, a person may change from full-time to part-time work, from an office job to home office and from the security of a big firm to the adventure of entrepreneurship.

Changes in the nature of work are also breaking down the rigid frontiers, which marked off the world of work. The traditionally distinct fields of work, education and leisure are now interwoven and coexist flexibly in a kind of triple helix of social life.

The emerging intangible and relational economy has a huge potential for growth because it is not bound by the constraints of material scarcity. However, the transition to the now economy is an open-ended process. The state has a key part to play in bringing it about. Governments can slow down the rate of change by making it more painful and more costly.

Obstacles to Change

Pessimistic scenarios are still plausible, such as that of an economy which generates few new jobs and is polarized between a small elite and the rest of the population who are marginalized and lie in precarious conditions. There is a big risk that this scenario will come to pass because current laws and regulations, as well as widespread pessimistic ideas about work, are powerful obstacles to change. Optimistic scenarios require a wholesale reform of institutional structures and profound changes in behaviour and attitudes. Such far-reaching changes often run into strong opposition from the social and political establishment and come up against the weight of psychological and social tradition. But the gamble of a new approach to work must be made if the transformation to the intangible economy is to succeed.

16

Population Growth and Jobs

Since mid-century, the world's labour force has more than doubled—from 1.2 billion people to 2.7 billion, outstripping the growth in job creation. As a result, the United Nations International Labour Organisation estimates that nearly 1 billion people, approximately 30 per cent of the global work force; are unemployed or underemployed (working but not earning enough to meet basic needs). Over the next half-century, the world will need to create more than 1.9 billion jobs—all of them in the developing world—just to maintain current levels of employment.

As economists often note, while population growth may boost labour demand (through economic activity and demand for goods), it will most definitely boost labour supply. During the next 50 years, almost 40 million people will enter the global labour force-defined as those between the ages of 15 and 65 seeking work-each year. Between 1995 and 2050, some 1.9 billion additional jobs will need to be created to absorb these new would-be workers. The most pressing needs will be found in the world's poorest nations—a sobering example of the vicious cycle linking poverty and population growth.

As the children of today represent the workers of tomorrow, the interaction between population growth and jobs is most acute in nations with young populations. Nations such as Peru, Mexico, Indonesia, and Zambia with more than half their population below the age of 25 will feel the burden of this labour flood. In the Middle East and Africa, 40 per cent of the population is under the age of 15. Since new entrants into the labour force were born at least 15 years ago, measures to reduce population growth have a delayed effect on the growth of the labour force, highlighting the urgency of taking action on population.

Nowhere is the employment challenge grater than in Africa, where at least 40 per cent of the population lives in absolute poverty. Although 8 million people entered the sub-Saharan work force in 1997, by 2030 this resource-scarce region will have to absorb more than 17 million new entrants each year. Over the next half-century, Nigeria's labour force is projected to grow by 246 per cent and Ethiopia's will soar by 337 per cent—both faster than growth of the general population. At current growth rates, the size of the labour force in sub-Saharan Africa will more than triple by 2050.

As a result of unprecedented population growth and increasing acceptance of female participation in the work force, the number of people seeking jobs in the Middle East and North Africa, a region already plagued by double-digit unemployment rates, will double in the next 50 years. In Algeria, where unemployment stands at 22 per cent, the labour force is growing at a staggering 4.2 per cent annually, and the number seeking work will more than double by 2050. Egypt alone will need to create 26 million more jobs by 2050 as its total population hits 115 million.

Nations throughout Asia will also see phenomenal increases in the numbers seeking work, including Pakistan, where the work force will grow from 70 million in 1998 to 205 million by 2050. Over the next 25 years, India will add nearly 10 million to its work force each year. During the same period, China will add nearly 6 million annually due to population growth alone, compounding the work short—ages caused by the current flood of migrants to China's coastal cities and by massive layoffs—estimated at more than 30 million—as state-run operations are scaled back.

Nations are hard-pressed to educate and train rapidly growing numbers of young people in marketable skills for the global workplace. Moreover, meeting the basic needs of a growing population draws scarce foreign exchange and other resources from investments in education and job creation. Throughout the world, young people entering the work force are increasingly faced with unemployment and social marginalisation. In most societies, unemployment rates for those under 25 are substantially higher than for older people.

Surplus farmland once served as a traditional source of employment for growing populations, as new land could be plowed to generate work and income. However, global percapita Greenland has dropped by half and considerably more in certain nations since 1950. Moreover, the machanisation of agriculture fuels the exodus of job seekers into the world's urban areas, where unemployment is often most acute heavily reliant on natural capital in the past, future job creation will require massive amounts of financial capital to jump-start the industrial and service sectors.

As the balance between the demand and supply of labour is tipped by population growth, wages—the price of labour-tend to decreases. And in a situation of labour surplus, the quality of jobs may not improve as fast for workers will settle for longer hours, fewer benefits and less control over work activities.

Employment is the key to obtaining food, housing, health services, and education, in addition to providing self-respect and self-fulfilment. Rising numbers of unemployed people could drive global poverty and hunger to precarious levels, fueling political instability.

17

State Trading Enterprises:

Existence of Monopolies is No Longer Justified

Agricultural state trading enterprises (STEs), used by some countries to control imports and encourage exports for non-commercial reasons, no longer have a place in global agriculture. STEs not only diminish benefits that other exporters expect in third-country markets, but they may create additional costs for producers, prompt predatory pricing practices that drive other exporters out of particular markets, and keep more producers in business and more land in production than would otherwise be the case.

The new disciplines on agricultural trade established in the Uruguay Round and the globalisation of international agricultural trade raise important questions about the role of state trading enterprises. Traditional reasons for maintaining STEs have included controlling imports, encouraging exports for non-commercial reasons (such as obtaining foreign exchange or removing surplus production), or establishing emergency food stockpiles.

However, rules prohibiting the maintenance of nontariff barriers through STEs and disciplines on export subsidies have eliminated most of their traditional purposes. As a consequence, agricultural STEs are a concern among many World Trade Organisation (WTO) members because of their potential to distort trade. Much of the concern arises from the substantial market power wielded by monopoly STE exporters and importers, commonly referred to as single-desk sellers and buyers. Some of the common characteristics of single-desk sellers and buyers are described here, along with some of the potential trade distortions that may result from the operation of the single-desk system.

Single-Desk Sellers

Single-desk sellers have common characteristics that may give them advantages in international trade and may lead to trade distortions. These include a lack of price transparency; government financial backing that may insulate them from the financial risks normally faced by other exporters; an ability to control procurement costs by maintaining monopsony control over purchases for domestic and export sales; an ability to "price discriminate" using cross-subsidisation, either between the domestic and export markets or between different buyers; and the ability to insulate produccers from market prices through price-pooling schemes. These characteristics and the distortions that they cause may diminish benefits that other exporters expect in third-country markets. Besides their potential to distort trade, single-desk sellers may create additional costs for producers or allocate inefficiencies caused by production driven by non-market price signals.

Monopoly authority and the lack of transparency in export pricing may provide single-desk sellers with greater pricing flexibility relative to private traders. In the private export trade, commodity prices, which are in effect "replacement values" for exported products, are quoted daily on various market exchanges. Private exporters have no choice but to buy their export supplies at a given market price, which is widely known in the trade and to governments. Single-desk sellers, in contrast, and not required to reveal their transaction prices. This may put them in a position to disguise procurement costs and subsequent export prices, particularly when export sales are subsidized through direct or indirect government subsidies.

Many single-desk sellers benefit from the financial backing of the Central Government, either through direct subsidies or from government guarantees. Because single-desk sellers are quasi-governmental entities or direct government agencies, their operational losses, which generally have been caused by pooling account deficits, are in most cases reimbursed by the federal government. The actual intervention by the government, or the functional equivalent afforded through the assurance of government intervention, shields producers from risk and encourages production because producers can rely on support when faced with reduced revenue from declining prices. This encourages higher levels of production than otherwise would occur.

Single-desk sellers are monopsony buyers for export and frequently monopolists for re-sales in the domestic market. As such, they can force producers to accept lower prices than might otherwise be possible under more competitive conditions. This is particularly important when a country exports a substantial share of total production. Producers, who frequently have no alternative crops to cultivate for geographic reasons, have no alternative but to sell to the single-desk exporter and take whatever price is offered, giving the single-desk seller wide flexibility in export pricing. Additionally, this control leaves open the opportunity for the single-desk seller to reduce, delay, or otherwise manipulate the price it pays producers to açquire supplies. The pricing power may be behind a host of many other practices that can lead to trade distortions, including price discrimination.

In world markets, where prices are normally outside the control of sellers in a particular country, the ability to price discriminate may represent a significant advantage for a single-desk seller. It may also lead to higher levels of imports into particular WTO member countries than world occur under perfectly competitive conditions. Price discrimination occurs when a single desk seller can differentiate its sales prices for comparable quality commodities between different destinations according to a buyer's ability to pay. The ability to discriminate allows a single-desk seller to maximize returns among a range of purchasers with different price elasticities by lowering prices to certain buyers without affecting its higher sales price in premium markets. Since single-desk sellers control their procurement costs, they have more power to raise and lower prices across different markets. If single-desk sellers are obliged to purchase all domestic production, the ability to price discriminate allows them to lower costs to whatever level is necessary to unload the product in foreign markets. Similarly, when single-desk sellers are driven by government policy objectives, such as maximizing production or exports rather than profits, sales in high-price markets can underwrite the sale of surplus products at uneconomical prices. Additionally, price discrimination encourages the use of predatory pricing practices, whereby a monopoly seller lowers its prices to drive other exporters out of a particular market. If successful, the single-desk seller can raise prices once the competition has been eliminated.

Price-pooling arrangements that are operated by single-desk sellers are intended to equalize payments to producers while minimizing the risk inherent in marketing their products. Under an pooling system, farmers deliver their product to a pool controlled by the single-desk seller in return for a initial payment. At the end of a marketing year, the single-desk seller tallies its total sales revenues and deducts marketing and other operational costs. The net revenue is then distributed to the producers. Under this system, each farmer, in effect, receives a blended price based on all sales for the year . Diversifying sales reduces the risk borne by producers, but it also leaves all export pricing decisions to the single-desk seller, which may set prices based on a range of government policy objectives. Although pooling helps reduce market risk for producers by acting to stabilize prices received during the marketing year, costs are inherent in the pooling system. For example, producers of higher-quality products, those that have achieved marketing efficiencies, or those that deliver products to the pool during a period of higher world prices are effectively penalized because they may receive a blended price derived from a lower-quality grade or from revenue generated by lower-priced sales. As a consequence, wealth is transferred from high-quality producers to lower-quality producers, which may keep more producers in business and more land in production than otherwise would be the case.

Single-desk Buyers

Single-desk buyers may be able to restrict or otherwise distort trade in several ways—lack of transparency, interference with end-users, enforcement of burdensome requirements on imported products, and procurement of emergency stockpiles. These and other purchasing and marketing practices may raise domestic prices and impair market access opportunities for exporters. Monopoly control over imports and the resulting market power of single-desk buyers may allow them to restrict access for imported products based on government-determined criteria, not on commercial considerations. This decision can be made without regard to prevailing world market conditions or domestic demand considerations. Ultimately, this control gives the single-desk buyer the flexibility to support internal prices and to otherwise regulate demand for imports.

Single-desk buyers generally provide insufficient transparency regarding their purchases and sales. Information on import pricing, resale pricing, requested grades and quality, and purchase quantities are not available to traders or the public. Lack of this information makes it difficult for exporters and domestic end-users to do business and may allow the single-desk buyer to disguise trade restrictions.

State control of marketing and distribution may interfere with end-user purchasing decisions—in contrast to direct contact between exporters and end-users, which allows the specification of grade and quality and leads to increased value of imported products to the end-user. This benefits end-users and consumers, but it can also benefit exporters who develop marketing relationships and receive higher prices by dealing with end-users who value the grade and quality of their products. However, when these decisions must go through single-desk importers, the importer can enforce other government policy objectives, such as discouraging imports of competitive grades and qualities or "luxury" imports, that restrict imports.

Single-desk buyers may be empowered to enforce burdensome requirements on imported products. Marketing control including control of internal marketing and distribution of imports, also gives the single-desk seller the ability to direct imports of inferior quality products that may be less competitive than domestically produced products. Retail pricing, promotion, and distribution of imported products are often controlled by the single-desk buyer. This may interfere with consumer preferences and efficient resource allocation, especially when marketing strategy is formulated by a state-controlled entity rather than a private firm that is subject to market competition.

18

Venture Capital for Small and Medium Business:

A Proposal for South-South Cooperation

Although great strides have been made in the last decade to help finance business start-ups for micro-enterprises in low-income countries (LICs), using models such as the Grameen Bank in Bangladesh and others, no similar initiative has been taken to help small and medium enterprises (SMEs) in these countries.

Development banks or other development finance institutions (DFIs) in developing countries are not really meant nor organised to serve the particular needs of their counties' SMEs. They are not only unable to draw on a local capital market to finance their operations, but they also lack the range of advisory services required by SMEs to submit bankable loan applications and are themselves ill-equipped to evaluate such applications. Consequently, they concentrate on a few large projects—preferably of the infrastructure type—for which they rely on the technical expertise of the foreign donors financing them or specially hired consultants.

In the absence of a realistic access to DFIs, SMEs have been constrained to seek their loans for new business ventures from commercial banks. The fact that since 1978 the World Bank has been challenging a large portion of its credit lines intended for SMEs through commercial banks rather than through DFIs, reflects the importance which donors attach to the role of LIC commercial banks as the principal intermediaries for SME lending.

Reasons for Failure of Traditional Banking Systems

However, there are several important reasons why commercial banks are ill-suited to perform this task. First and foremost, the banking systems of these countries were conceived during a period when most investment capital was provided by the government, usually drawing on foreign aid. Thus, even in those LICs which had not entirely succumbed to the socialist ideology in the sense of eliminating all private enterprise, commercial banks continue to limit their credit activity largely to self-liquidating, low-risk credits seldom exceeding 12 months's duration, preferably conventional trade credits. Secondly, even in the exceptional cases where commercial banks in these countries entertain applications for medium-term credits to finance the launching of a small manufacturing project, they will normally demand ironclad collateral in the forms of liens on real-estate and/or personal guarantees by friends and relatives with similar backing, unless the applicant is a well-known customer of the bank

Thirdly, with their overriding concern for profitability, most LIC commercial banks tend to like upon business start-up loans to SMEs as being too risky and/or administratively too costly to handle in relation to the loan amounts involved. For these reasons, commercial banks in these countries are unlikely to establish in-house facilities to meet the specific needs of SMEs, such as helping them in project preparation and market analysis. Last but not least, factors such as the project's development orientation" (e.g. its important substitution and export potential, its ability to increase productivity and its employment generation features) do not enter into the calculations of commercial banks which will orient their actions towards "bottom line" results and risk minimisation. Under the circumstances, most commercial banks are not inclined to become directly involved in project supervision, as long as their customer's repayment records are satisfactory.

Credit for SMEs

Whereas new approaches have been developed over the last decade by various development assistance agencies to help up-grade commercial banks' staff capability, especially in advising SME borrowers in such matters as project formulation and market analysis as well as improving their loan repayment capacity, only recently has an effort been made to find ways and means of making investment capital available to SME entrepreneurs for launching new businesses. In some LICs, lines of credit have been established by multilateral or bilateral banks from which loan capital can be sought for such projects, but only seldom has genuine risk (i.e., equity) capital been made available and when some only through the donors' own agencies. The interest rate charged by the local banks for administering loans from these credit lines in local currency are generally at par with existing commercial rates, which tend to be prohibitive for a new venture of the type being promoted. These high rates are due to several factors, including (a) the local rates of inflation and the consequent devaluation risks, (b) the high risk factor of the new enterprises with little or no collateral and credit standing, and (c) the lack of experience of bank staff in the evaluation of loan requests submitted to them for unfamiliar projects.Significantly, most international DFIs are loath to lower interest rates to be applied on loans financed by their credit lines, lest they be accused of unfair competition on the local financial markets.

Incentives Ineffective in Attracting Foreign Investors

Although many international conferences, investment promotion meetings and other fora have been staged by UN bodies and donor groups to generate private investor interest in the LICs, these efforts have proved largely ineffectual. While much has been done by LIC governments in recent years to create a more attractive "enabling environment" for private investment, these incentives have been necessary but not sufficient to convince developed—country enterprises or investors to assume the necessary risks, with the exception of selected sectors such as mineral extraction, tourism and a narrow range of exportable consumer goods, such as out-of-season fruits and vegetables, and tropical products such as cocoa and certain spices. Even public support for project preparation has ultimately failed to provide preparation private business in industrial countries the incentives needed to take an active role in a broadly-based economic development of LICs.

The bottom line for potential investors in LICs is constituted by the profits which their investment will yield within a reasonable period of time, under conditions which offer a reasonable amount of political and legal stability. So far, these basic conditions have not been met on the whole. In the new global economy with its almost total reliance on free market principles and the ability to choose investment sites freely, the choice is not likely to fall on the LICs, but rather on a small number of more advanced developing countries, apart from the industrial countries themselves.

South-to-South Technological/Commercial Cooperation

While the inherent disadvantages faced by LICs in competing for foreign investment capital are too great to be overcome by a magic panacea, any attempt at a solution must include measures designed to mobilise the entrepreneurial abilities and dynamism available in existing and potential SMEs engaged in production of a variety of goods destined for the broad consumer market at home and abroad. In most LICs such existing or potential SMEs need to access affordable foreign technologies, i.e., the machinery and the technological know-how required to install and make the machinery function. One of the prime sources of such technologies for LICs can be found in enterprises in South/Southeast Asia and China, countries that have only recently graduated from the LIC status (or have not yet done so but have nevertheless managed to create a modern industrial sector within their overall state of underdevelopment and poverty). The concretisation of transfers of technology from these countries to the LICs is especially affected by the financing problems described above, because in the normal case neither one of the potential partners can afford the necessary venture, even though they can and will invest their know-how, time and very often land, buildings and infrastructure. This problem is much less acute in the case of the more expensive, and hence often unaffordable "Northern" technologies, where the technology provider finds it easier to mobilise start-up capital from its won resources or by borrowing from his commercial bank against his firms' overall credit line.

The underlying economic rationale in favour of such South-to South, company-to company transfers of production technology argues that Asian firms can help launch industrial start-ups in these countries far more cheaply and quickly than the more sophisticated companies from the North. By offering labour-intensive rather than capital-intensive production machinery accompanied by vitally needed on the-job training, back-up managerial and maintenance follow-up at a fraction of the cost of Northern firms, Asian companies' Cooperation can spell the difference between a successful business start-up and a failed one. Furthermore Asian-sourced machinery can be operated at production scales corresponding to the reduced market requirements and limited purchasing power of most LIC markets.

In view of the above described financing problems faced by South-to-South deals, it is proposed that a Venture Capital Fund be established specializing in the provision of equity capital for joint ventures (JVs) among SMEs in various LICs. In many cases the existence of such a FUND—Which might be called the Venture Capital Fund or simply (VENCAP)—will spell the difference between business proposals that are still-born for want of the required initial financing, and profitable ventures which are launched thanks to the missing—if minority—equity contribution from the fund.

Characteristics of the FUND

The proposed VENCAP would be expected to be an active participant in the project in which it will invest, sharing its financial and strategic vision with the invested firm. To this end, it must have access to experienced project evaluation specialists with intimate knowledge of conditions in low-income countries in general, and the project and its promoters in particular. As might be expected, the FUND would concentrate its resources in early-state financing, rather than in plant expansion or replacement, inasmuch as the projects likely to be the most profitable are the new ones which will normally start from empty factory buildings and offices, where only a minimum amount of production equipment if any, is normally usable for the operation of the new JV.

The FUND would limit its participation to joint ventures in which firms of at least two developing countries hold equity stakes, although firms from developed countries might also participate. The FUND would limit its participation to production JVs whose total initial capital would not exceed a given sum to be determined. Its own participation would in turm also be limited by a relative ceiling per venture i.e., a maximum percentage of the total capital. This combination would implicitly set an absolute ceiling to the FUND's participation in any given JV.

Success and Selection Criteria

The number of proposed projects must be sufficient to allow the FUND to pick and choose the best A good ratio of applications to acceptances might be in the range of 10:1 Whereas commercial viability will constitute the first and foremost selection criterion, every effort would be made to select projects which have a strong development character, are environmentally friendly and/or involve production technologies which are deemed to be vital and critical to the recipient country's current socio-economic needs. Thus, preference would be given to sectors such as (a) food processing (b) Water purification, (c) renewable energy (d) agricultural development, and (e) light engineering. In all cases, the emphasis would be on cost-effective, labour-intensive production technologies.

The FUND's ability to divest itself of its participation at a profit will be the ultimate test of the FUND's success. Ideally, the FUND should be able to do this within a maximum of one or two years, so as to enable it to effectively cycle its resources to other equally meritorious projects.

Proposals for VENCAP's Organisational Structure

Besides being run by an experienced FUND manager, VENCAP would be assisted in its investment decisions by National Advisory Committees (NACs), which would be established in all participating LICs and would be composed of prominent business persons, professional men and women and financiers. These NACs would be chaired by an experienced consultant/consulting firm selected by the FUND. No member of the NAC having business or family links with the person or firm applying for equity finacing would participate in the evaluation procedure. VENCAP would be represented on the Boards of Directors of the firms in which it has acquired minority stakes through one or several members of the relevant NAC. The FUND itself would be run by a Board of Directors in which all of the major investors would be represented (and possibly some NGOs PVOs).

Follow-up

It is hoped that this article will provoke sufficient interest to justify the convening of an international meeting of aid agency officials and experts to study the ideas set forth above, so as to facilitate VENCAP's formal launching as an operative force. The need is there, the customer are there, the goodwill is there, only the financing and the organisation are lacking!

19

Taking a Lead in the Fight Against Poverty?

World Bank and IMF Speed Implementation of their New Strategy

A change in development policy strategy in the poorest countries is at present being prepared with incredible speed. The IMF-style structural adjustment programmers that have been criticised for many years are being scrapped. The countries are now to take their own decisions on their paths to development. Their governments will no longer formulate poverty reduction programmes top-down, but in an intensive and long-term dialogue with societal groups and organisations. Governments and institutions of the North commit themselves to supporting these processes, such as by debt relief on an unprecedented scale. Dream or reality?

New Strategy Paper

Behind this euphoria lines a new abbreviation, PRSP, standing for Poverty Reduction Strategy Paper, which the IMF and World Bank invented last year. The G-7 countries in Cologne not only announced debt relief for the Heavily Indebted Poor Countries (HIPCs) but also demanded that it must serve above all for poverty reduction. The PRSP concept was then presented at the annual conference of the two Bretton Woods organisations.

The most important principles of the new "super weapon" in the fight against poverty are:

- PRSPs are papers, which describe the medium-term development paths of the poorest countries of the

South, particularly their strategies to combat poverty, and by this means enlist international support. A PRSP is not only the prerequisite for granting debt forgiveness in the context of the HIPC initiative. It is also necessary for all new IMF and World Bank loans to the so-called IDA countries, the some 70 poorest countries that receive concessional loans from the World Banks's International Development Agency (IDA). According to the World Bank, PRSPs should also be required for all future pledges of bilateral development assistance.

- Not only social sector programmes, but also the economic and financial policies of the developing countries are in future to be aimed at fighting poverty. Previously, the IMF always pronounced that a growth-oriented national economy and a far-reaching integration in the world market would have a trickle-down effect and also benefit the poor. Now the poor are to be asked what policies can help materially to improve their situation.
- PRSPs are to be developed on the basis of self-responsible country ownership. Accordingly, development and structural adjustment strategies are no longer to be developed by the Washington finance institutions, but the countries themselves.
- The heading "country ownership" is to underline that not only governments are called upon, PRSPs should come into being in a participatory process. That means involvement of trade unions, NGOs cooperatives, associations, grass roots, groups, political parties and parliaments. A country's PRSP should be developed in a societal debate, a dialogue between governments on one side and parliamentary, private sector and civil society on the other.

Rhetoric or Reality?

Are PRSPs the expression of a change of paradigm? In brief, if all what the papers contain is implemented in a consistent and wide-ranging, way, the chances of achieving it are good but there are a number of open questions. The answers to them will have a bearing on success or failure.

- Is the IMF really changing its policy on the poorest countries or merely wrapping it old policy in new words? The growing critism of the IMF in recent years strengthened latterly by the evaluation of the ESAF (Enhanced Structural Adjustment Facility) programmes, which once again proved their blatant weaknesses called for reaction and is now triggering changes—real or only rhetorical? There will be no more old-style ESAF loans based on macroeconomic structural adjustment programmes. But the credit line remains, and is now called the Poverty Reduction and Growth Facility (PRGF). This will be granted on the basis of the PRSPs, which in each case must also be accepted by the IMF board of directors. How much influence will the IMF have on the design of the PRSPs? What happens if a government choose macroeconomic strategies combat poverty which go against previous IMF policy? Open questions. Moreover, there is still no answer to the question of why the IMF is at all coming on with long-term and low-interest lines of credit in the poorest countries.

Mixed Feelings with Regard to World Bank Role

- Will the World Bank use the PRSP process to expand its own institutional power further? NGOs in the North and South are viewing this with mixed feelings. Many welcome the fact that for the moment the World Bank appears to be asserting itself against its twin, the IMF. On the other hand, 50 years of experience with World Bank strategies have certainly not strengthened their trust in the Bank's ability to make a convincing fight against poverty. That is why the EURODAD network also questions the role of the World Bank (and the IMF) in the PRSP process. It says the papers should not be presented to the two financial institutions, whose power over the development strategies of countries of the South thus would increase further. Rather, PRSPs should for example, be laid before a Round Table of all donors chaired by the United Nations Development Programme (UNDP).

Ownership

- The principles of developing countries being responsible for their own development strategies are as old as it is—in theory—right. There have been frequent complaints about shortcomings in ownership. But now, after decades of development strategies being set and structural adjustment programmes being dictated from outside, the governments of the poorest countries, which in many cases have only weak institutional capacities, can hardly taken on sole respnsibility overnight. In addition, of course, not a few of the countries are ruled by corrupt political elites (promoted from outside over decades) that give little reason to hope they would immediately switch to poverty reduction polities. Scepticism and critical observation is justified even if there is no alternative to governments of the south taking over greater responsibility.
- Civil society actors are now asked to help out in particular in those countries whose governments appear to be less trustwothy. A nice idea that has little to do with real life. Civil society actors in developing countries in general and in the poorest countries in particular are extraordinarily weak institutions which in many cases are totally dependent on financing from the North.

The civil society landscape in other countries is even weaker. However, social actors in many countries could make useful contributions to developing sustainable strategies. But that calls for meaningful and lasting support, including financial support, capacity building, and in some countries also political pressure to gain scope for societal engagement.

It is reasonable that not only the World Bank and other official donors but also, and above all, the northern NGO partners of these actors are now giving much thought to how civil societies in the south can be strengthened.

Participation?

Even assuming there were civil society actors capable of dialogue, that does not clarify what participation in the PRSP process is really supposed to mean. Is civil society only to be listened to, or can it if necessary refuse to approve a PRSP? What impact would a refusal have on acceptance of the document by the IMF and World Bank and other donor? And in view of the great time pressure, will civil society be at all able to formulate discuss and feed their positions into the process? It could be of decisive importance for the current debate on the PRSP model to delink the urgently needed debt relief from drawing up a PRSP programme, which simply needs more time. For example, it is conceivable that there would be no great problems in granting a country a moratorium on debt servicing so long as a PRSP process is continuing and then for giving debt when it is completed. That would ease the time problem for NGOs and at the same time maintain pressure on governments actually to arrive at poverty reduction strategies that were developed in a participatory process.

Other Causes of Poverty in Developing Countries

The entire current process is focused on the countries of the south, their governments and societies. That diverts attention from the responsibility of the donors and creditors. Not only that the IMF's structural adjustment programmes to date have been counterproductive for fighting poverty (why does the IMF not admit that openly just for once?) Not only that the now promised debt reliefs are coming much too late the debt crisis of the poorest countries was deplored decades ago!). The present strategy also ignores various other exogenous causes of poverty in the South. What impacts do the finance and trade policies of northern countries have on the modest attempts to enable sustainable development in the South? What consequences will the continuing cutting of development budgets have on the South (no one anyway ventures to talk nowadays about the old 0.7 per cent ODA-GNP ratio) Fort the donors and creditors to now pass the buck of sole responsibility to the governments of the South and present themselves in the background as noble do-gooders may be a successful strategy in terms of domestic politics, but not an acceptable one for development policy.

20

What was Wrong with Structural Adjustment

In Defence of a Much-Maligned Strategy

After decades of stranded development theories, ideologies and paradigms, structural adjustment", with its demands for clean fiscal policy and an end to uneconomic state enterprises, political privileges, market and exchange rate intervention and corruption, entered the aid arena like a refreshing dawn after long night of frustrating dreams. Only the "old guard" of planned economy advocates and jealous academicians who had missed the boat were able to shut their eyes to the moral and economic justification of this liberating break-though international development policy spearheaded by the Breton Woods institutions then steered by some exceptionally courageous economists.

Reaction To Saps

As with any revolution, defeat is awaiting the pioneers at the hands of political power greed, reactionary tactics by the formerly privileged and academic envy. The principal device serving the reactionary forces as a lever of influence on the mood of the "development community" has been the identification and dramatisation of new pockets or strata of (principally urban) poverty allegedly created by structural adjustment measures, while shunning the much broader-based rise in economic activity, real incomes and sense of fair reward in the overall society, especially the rural population. That the hardship experienced by urban poor, formerly privileged under consumer price control and import subsidies to the debit depressed farm prices or maintained by grossly over expanded public payrolls, was only laying open the camouflaged erosion of the economy and near-bankruptcy of governments and public enterprises, was conveniently downplayed.

These reactionary howls were to be expected. Not that they met the entirely innocent. There had been naively sweeping, overly assuming demands by some structural adjustment missions. But an intellectually vigorous and dynamic "development community" would have coped with the ensuing opposition, strengthened the analytical and monitoring capacities and the political will to endure also rocky roads and bitter medicines on the way to a healthier base. Instead institutional rivalry, political opportunism and emotive populism were thriving. In a way, the "development community" behaved as if it did not want its patient to become able to stand on his own feet and eventually steal its raison d'être.

Worst, the Bretton Woods Institutions themselves, partly under the pressure of the emotive opposition described above fell to the temptation to rescue their lending volume, which was threatened by the frugality dictated to Third World public budgets under structural adjustment recipes, through hardship-easing loans. They thereby corrupted their creation in using it to reinforce their indispensability. As a consequence it soon turned out that some of the most obedient loan takers under structural adjustment terms experienced sharply rising indebtedness, exploited as a disqualifying symptom by the anti-structural adjustment camp

Whatever the opinions on structural adjustment policies, the commitment to the principles of "good governance" has come to stay, at least on paper, as an almost standard conditionally for official development aid from OECD donor countries. The realisation, matured in the implementation of structural adjustment programmes, that not the quantity of aid, but the quality of Third World government determines the positive or negative course of development, may be regarded as the most valuable fruit of the decades-old policy debate in the 'development community". And the use of aid a pressure or bribing factor towards "good governance" as foreign aid's least disputable purpose.

Out of the Limelight

Nothing, however, must be taken for granted. Achievement breeds its challenge! Structural adjustment, though in essence hardly disputable has been pushed out of the limelight and replaced by the oldest actor in the company, eradication of poverty, twinned with an equally perpetual endeavour at the macro-level: debt-forgiveness. This falling back to square one in donors approach to the problems of the south, i.e., the call to alleviate poverty and priorities direct efforts to this end above all other developmental efforts—does it indicate a sell-out of constructive ideas in the "development community"? Has any noteworthy progress been achieved in the past by this approach?

By telling a frugally toiling but independent subsistence farmer that internationally his condition is classed as "poverty", deserving compassion and support by the world community and cancellation of his debts, one can hardly expect a sustainable improvement in his output, satisfaction, or self-respect and even less, when he realises that the help principally provides jobs, fringe benefits and self-importance to a gamut of intermediaries, at home and abroad.

What do those poverty advocates (the"Lords of poverty") really know about the resources, life managements, value systems and ambitions of those they generalize by the billions? The great variance in the conception of life situations, from different external viewpoints.

What the aid system can do for these rural populations classed as "poor"/"underprivileged"/"exploited", is press for justice, i.e., "good governance". The achievement of structural adjustment policy through e.g. abolishing official price and exchange rate distortions, import subsidies and exploitative state agencies, has brought massive income improvement for peasant populations, i.e. the majority of LDC inhabitants, in dimensions unreachable by whatsoever direct "attack" on rural "poverty". What people want is not being benevolently treated as poor, but being justly rewarded for their work, i.e., by access to the unmanipulated market of their output. Slackening on structural adjustment/"good governance" conditionally under the present "10 year itch" for paradigm change means foregoing much of the potential opportunities for undoing injustice and exploitation of the masses. It should be clear where priority focus should be placed in ODA policy.

Small is Not Beautiful

The direct attack on "poverty", orchestrated by the Bretton Woods institutions under their freshly launched Poverty Reduction Strategy Paper (PRSP) campaign, is being rightly regarded as primarily an NGO domain, since most activities are expected to be carried out at local community level. This would require careful screening and coordinating of NGO activities and their integration via gradual expansion of their experience. But "small" is not "beautiful" for the development financing institution. Disbursement needs are pressing, calling for the new paradigm to quickly provide channels for another wave of loans to the "IDA Countries". Their problem of heavy indebtedness, which would principally exclude most of them from any new loan consideration, shall be solved with one stroke (which only the well-cushioned development bureaucracy can afford); debt relief against presentation of country PRSPs by the respective governments. NGOs are expected of play in the system especially the knowledge gap about the "poor" people's real wants and needs NGOs will naturally be tempted by such expansionary boost to their involvement (referred to sarcastically as their philanthropic empire" by an African conference participant), but this will not be conducive to quality and accountability of their performance, which ideally should be based on piivate sponsorship in combination with strong target-group provided self-help components.

Patience and Self-Restraint

Local knowledge and initiatives cannot be obtained under time pressure. "The grass does not grow faster by being pulled" When will the "development community" learn patience and self-restraint in the approach to LDC's capacity for constructive absorption of aid programmes accompanied by a genuine sense of ownership?

After all these deliberations, how shall development policy be shaped in order to better correspond with reality, without sinking deeper into hypocrisy and frustration?

To come back to the opening question: what was wrong with "structural adjustment"? Nothing was wrong with its intent. In fact this was very right and long overdue. Its implementation, however, lacked patience, perseverance and solid support from the development community, apart from its being corrupted as a vehicle for expansionary lending policy. If aid is meant to not be an end in itself, then structural adjustment policy needs constant reinforcement, underpinned by strict lending discipline. There should be an end to irresponsible lending and easy escape from its consequences by wholesome periodic debt relief burdened on the international tax-paying community. No ODA, either loans or grants, should be made available to governments who are not in active process of implementing "good governance" principles. A monitoring unit, reporting to the donor community on government performance in regard to its "-good government"? Structural adjustment commitment, should be maintained in each and receiving country by "donor consortia" comprising all locally represented bilateral and multilateral development organisations currently extending technical, financial or material assistance to the country.

In order to accommodate the poverty focus without diluting the necessary structural adjustment orientation of ODA, a division of activity-focus between the latter and the NGO sector would seem to be advantageous.

- ODA, limited to the countries abiding to structural adjustment/"good governance" conditionally, with focus concentration on sustainable physical, social and economic infrastructure principally at national and regional level, public management training, higher education and research, consultant and senior adviser services.
- The NGO sector, principally funded by private sponsorship, united to structural adjustment conditionally (but preferably grafted on local self-help

initiative), with focus concentration on the "Third World "poor", i.e., mostly at rural community and low-income township level, for amelioration of living conditions and local resource utilisation.

Strengthening of linkages between the NGO sector and the UN Technical Agencies to mutual benefit: NGOs in need of professional information, evaluation and advice, of forum for discussion to find an actively supportive window at the agencies; the latter to maintain and develop field contact of research and policy generation, not least as a substitute for their declining project work (giving way to greater concentration on their global functions i.e., serving as information, policy initiation, and coordination/ negotiation centre on topics of global concern such as e.g. : human rights, global monetary and trade systems, tropical forest and global marine resources, global and regional health threats, international standards.)

In conclusion, it can be called to mind aid and its institutions have no claim for permanence. They are justified only as temporary functions in a phasing-out process of self-help support. Any claim for unlimited continuity would breed lasting infantilisation.

21

Consumption Bomb

It is three decades since we passed the peak world population growth rate of 2.04 per cent. Annual additions too are now a decade pas t their peak of 86 Million a year. They are currently running at 78 Million a year and are heading downwards. A peak in total numbers, however, still lies at least four or five decades ahead. On the UN Population Division's 1998 projections, the total is likely to reach 8.9 billion in 2050. The long range medium projection, which has not been updated since 1996, expects world population to level out at just under 11 billion in 2200 AD.

However, this is based on assumptions that are increasingly questionable. More and more countries are reaching levels of female fertility that are not enough for replacement—below 2.1 children over the lifetime of each women. At the latest count there are 61 countries in this category. Of this 23 had very low fertility, below 1.5.

The situation is unprecedented in times of global peace on economic growth. The UN medium projection assumes that where fertility is very low it will rise again to 1.7-1.9 children per woman, In all countries where fertility is currently above replacement level of 2.1, it assumes that it will not fall below that level.

Yet fertility has fallen below replacement level in so many countries, which such different cultures and different stages of economic growth, that is increasingly looking as if low fertility may be here to stay. If this became the case, then world population may peak at some where between 8 and 9 billion. There after it may well begin to decline. The 1996 long range low projection has world population falling to 5.6 billion in 2100 AD.

None of this means that reproductive rights should have lower priority in future. Their contribution to the health and welfare of women and children and clear. Many poor countries in Africa and South Asia face huge population increases which will be hard to accommodate without major problems of land and water scarcity. In these areas reproductive rights receive a very high priority.

Increasingly our concern must focus on consumption, and how we can cope with the effects of its inexorable increase. Over the past 25 years world population increased by 53 per cent, but world consumption per person (Measured by income) by only 39 per cent. Assume that consumption per person will rise 100 per cent, while population will rise by only half that amount. As time goes on the preponderance of consumption will increase more and more.

There is a crucial difference between population and consumption aspirations. If fully assured of children's survival most people have quite modest desire for family size. But their desire to consume knows no upper bounds. As wealth increases, people double-up their possessions; two or three cars, two bathrooms, two rooms with all contents, two or three holidays a year.

Appliances improve every year and old ones "need" replacing. New needs are created that never existed before. Globalisation is making products cheaper than ever. TVs are no longer uncommon even in African shanty towns. The number of households is increasing as people live longer and family breakdown becomes more common. Smaller households consume considerably more per per cent than large. Moreover, consumption is politically very difficult to restrain. No one can get elected promising people they can earn and spend less, or re-elected if they fulfil their promises.

In view of this much of the burden of reducing our environmental impact will rest on technology. Technology will have to deliver major shifts in improving resource productivity, and in reducing the amount of waste we create. All our institutions and forms of management which affect technology will need to be geared to this end.

In some areas the record has been good and looks likely to remain so. Productivity has kept up with demand in the case of resources that are traded on markets, and that are under the direct control of people or companies affected by shortages or prices. Global food production has kept pace with demand: although land and cereal production per person has declined, average intakes of calories and protein have continued to improve and are at record levels. Malnutrition persists, but this is due to poverty and landlessness, not to the inability of the world to produce enough food. We have not encountered any limiting shortage of any key mineral resources or of energy. Nor are we likely to, because we continually economise and find substitutes, there has been a gradual reduction in the material used for each unit of production.

The prospects are much worse for resources that are not traded on markets or subject to sustainable management, as yet. These include groundwater, state forests, ocean fish, biodiversity in general. They include communal waste sinks like rivers, lakes and oceans, and the global atmosphere. In all of these areas it looks likely that things will get quite a lot worse before they get better.

These kinds of resources and sinks are not under the direct control of people affected by shortage or damage. People wishing to change the way a common resource or sink is used or managed have to pass through the legal or political system. They must organise, take out lawsuits against polluters, pressurise legislators and so on. Political responses are typically slow. Usually the majority of voters have to be convinced of the need for action before politicians will risk taking action. Even then powerful and rich vested interest will lobby hard for the status quo, and will often succeed in frustrating changes that are desired by a global majority. American's coal, oil, and car lobbies have stood in the way of any significant US commitment to reduce carbon dioxide output, and the US is the world's largest emitter of carbon dioxide.

Usually there has to be very wide spread and very visible environmental damage before action is taken. The thinning of the ozone layer fitted that category well and the response was swift. North Atlantic fishing reached that point in the 1990s, yet politicians shied away from taking adequate action until the last moment: fishing stocks plummeted and there was massive job loss. Global warming is still long way from the damage being widespread enough, and attributable clearly enough to human activities, for politicians to be ready to speed up the move into renewable energy.

The question with the common resources and sinks is always: will we react in time? The answer is all the more difficult because we usually don't know in advance what is "in time." Many critical changes are subject to threshold effects. When a certain point is crossed, very sudden and disastrous change can occur with little warning. In many cases we do not know where the thresholds lie.

Prudence dictates a preventive approach—a stitch in time saves nine. But the history of environmental problems shows that politicians rarely act decisively until the brink is reached, and it will always be touch and go whether we are pushed over it or not.

22

The Population Challenge

During the last half-century world population has more than doubled, climbing from 2.5 billion in 1950 to 5.9 billion in 1998. Those of us born before 1950 are members of the first generation to witness a doubling of world population. Stated otherwise, there has been more growth in pollution since 1950 than during the 4 million years since our early ancestors first stood upright.

This unprecedented surge in population combined with rising individual consumption, is pushing our claims on the planet beyond its natural limits. Water tables area falling on every continent as demand exceeds the sustainable yield of aquifers. Eventual aquifer depletion will bring irrigation cutbacks and shrinking harvests. Our growing appetite for seafood has pushed oceanic fisheries to their limits and beyond. Collapsing fisheries tell us we can go no further. The Earth's temperature is rising, promising changes in climate that we cannot even anticipate. We are triggering the greatest extinction of plant and animal species since the dinosaurs disappeared. As our numbers go up, their numbers go down.

These effects of population growth are relatively recent, but assertions that population growth could affect human welfare are not. In 1798 Thomas Malthus, a British clergyman and intellectual, warned in his famous piece, *An Essay on the Principles of Population*, of the tendency for population to grow exponentially while food supply grew arithmetically. He saw a world where human numbers would continually press against available food supplies.

During the 200 years since Malthus issued his warning, famine has visited countries as diverse as Ireland and India, Ethiopia and China. Indeed, despite the near-tripling of the world grain harvest since 1950 the hungry and malnourished in 1998 number an estimated 840 million-nearly as many people as lived in the world when Malthus penned his essay.

But the nature of famine has changed. Whereas it was once geographically defined by areas of poor harvests, today famine is economically defined by low income in those segments of society that lack the purchasing power to buy enough food. Famine concentrated among the poor is less visible than the more traditional version but is no less real.

In addition to checks imposed by food shortages, there is evidence that other checks on population growth are now emerging, such as new infectious diseases, including AIDS, Ethnic conflicts within societies, such as Rwanada and the Sudan, are also taking a growing toll. Water shortages on a scale that would deprive people of enough water to produce food could undermine governments.

The evidence gathered here indicates that the rapid population growth prevailing in a majority of the world's countries is not going to continue much longer. Either countries will get their act together, shifting quickly to smaller families, or death rates will rise from one or more of the stresses just mentioned. As human demands press against more and more of the Earth's limits, the questions is not whether population growth will slow, but how. Will it be because countries do it humanely by shifting quickly to smaller families? Or because they fail to do so, and nature ruthlessly imposes its own constraints? In a world facing many challenges as it prepares to enter the next century, this may be the most challenging of all.

Estimates of future numbers are based on the latest United Nations population projections, using their medium level figures. Under this scenario, world population will grow from 6.1 billion in 2000 to 9.4 billion in 2050 a gain of 3.3 billion. The other two U.N. projections put global population in 2050 as high as 11.2 billion or as low as 7.7 billion. While the medium scenario is judged by the U.N. demographers as the one most likely to materialize, it is not an inevitable population part for the next century. Indeed, because the projections are based exclusively on demographic assumptions and do not take into account the environmental limits to carrying capacity, they should be viewed as a first pass rather than the final word on estimates of future population.

We use the medium-level projections to give an idea of the strain this "most likely" outcome would place on ecosystems and governments, and the urgent need to break from the business-as-usual scenario. The mid-level projected growth in population of 3.3 billion by 2050 is very close to the growth that will have occurred between 1950 and 2000, some 3.6 billion. But there is one difference. During the half-century now ending, the growth occurred in both industrial and developing countries. During the next half-century, the entire burden of the projected increase of 3.3 billion will be in developing countries, many of which are hard-pressed to satisfy even existing demands on resources. In fact, the population of the industrial world is expected to decline slightly.

The annual rate of world population growth reached its historical high in 1964 at 2.2 per cent. Since then, it has been slowly declining, dropping to 1.4 per cent in 1998. Despite the falling rate of growth the number of people aged each year increased from 72 million in 1964 to the all-time peak of 87 million in 1990. Since then the annual addition has also declined, falling to 80 million in 1997, where it is projected to remain for the next two decades before starting to decline.

The population projections for individual countries vary more widely than at any time in history. At mid-century populations were growing everywhere, but today they have stabilized in some 32 countries, while they continue to expand in some countries at 3 per cent or more a year, Indeed, the world can be divided demographically into two camps: countries that have achieved population stability or are well on the way to doing so, and those that have not.

With the exception of Japan, all the nations in the first camp are in Europe. And all are industrial countries, The populations of some countries, including Russia, Japan, and Germany, are actually projected to decline some what over the next half-century. In addition to the 32 countries, containing 12 per cent of world population, that have stabilized their populations, in another 39 countries fertility has dropped to replacement level (roughly two children per couple) or below. Among the countries in this category are China and the United States the first and third largest countries, which together contain 26 per cent of the world's people.

Although fertility in these 39 countries has fallen below replacement level, their populations have not yet stabilized because there is a disproportionately large number of young people moving into the reproductive age group. Thus even if they hold their fertility at replacement level, population may continue to grow for several decades before it stabilizes. It was this realisation that led China nearly 20 years ago to shift its goal from a two-child to a one-child family. Leaders in Beijing realized that, if they did not do this they would be faced with adding the equivalent of another India to their population—a development they considered potentially disastrous for their people.

In contrast to this group some countries are projected to triple their populations over the next half-century. For example, Ethiopia's current population of 62 million will more than triple, as it climbs to 213 million in 2050 Pakistan's population is projected to go from 148 million to 357 million, surpassing that of the United States before 2050 today to 339 million, giving it more people in 2050 than there were in all of Africa in 1950. From an environmental Vantage point, considering particularly the availability of water and cropland, it is unlikely that the projected population increases for these three countries, and other countries with similar projected gains, will materialise.

As hard as it is to imagine the addition of another 3.3 billion people to the world's population, it is even more difficult to understand the effects of adding such numbers. As we look back over the last half-century, we see that World lumber use more than doubled, paper use increased nearly sixfold, grain consumption nearly tripled, water use tripled, and fossil fuel burning increased some fourfold. The relative contribution of population growth and rising affluence to the growth in demand for various resources varies widely. With lumber use, most of the doubled use is accounted for by population growth. With paper, in contrast, rising affluence is primarily responsible for the growth in use.

One way to understand the consequences of future population growth is to contrast some of the key trend projected for the next half-century with those of the as one. For example, we have seen a new fivefold growth in the oceanic fish catch and a doubling in the supply available per person, but biologists now believe we may have "hit the wall" in oceanic fisheries and that the oceans cannot sustain a catch any larger than today's. Thus people born today are likely to see the catch per person cut in half during their lifetimes.

Grainland per person has been shrinking since midcentury, but the drop projected for the next 50 years means the world will have less grainland per person than India has today. Future population growth is likely to reduce this key number in many societies to the point where they will no longer be enable to feed themselves. Countries such as Ethiopia, India, Nigeria, and Pakistan will see grainland per person shrink by 2050 to less than one tenth of a hectare (one fourth of an acre) far smaller than a typical suburban building lot in the United States.

Given that at the amount of fresh water produced each year is essentially fixed by nature, the water available, per person has shrunk steadily as a result of population growth, leading to sever water shortages in some areas. Countries now experiencing these shortages include China and India, along with scores of smaller ones. As irrigation water is diverted to industrial and residential uses.

The challenge to governments presented by continuing rapid population growth is not limited to natural resources. It also includes education, housing, and jobs. During the last half-century the world has fallen further and further behind in creating jobs, leading to record levels of unemployment and under employment. Unfortunately over the next 50 years the number of entrants into the job market will be even greater. Few things threaten the political stability of a country as much as growing ranks of unemployed young people.

As noted earlier, the U.N. population projections cited here are based on exclusively demographic assumptions, which are not related to the population carrying capacity of local eco systems. These projections are purely statistical, based on historical data on fertility, mortality, and average life span and assumptions about future trends.

Based on the analysis in it, I conclude that the medium projection of 9.4 billion people in 2050 which U.N. demographers consider to be the most problem is unlikely to materialize. Rather the world is more likely to follow a path closer to the low population projection of 7.7 billion by mid-century.

What is less clear is whether we will move to the lower trajectory because countries with rapid pollution growth quickly shift to smaller families or because they fail to do so and the resulting inability to manage threats from disease, spreading hunger, or social disintegration leads to rising death rates. '

23

Winners and Losers:
The WTO and the Developing Countries

The World Trade Organisation (WTO) began work on January 1, 1995. The new international body's tasks include implementing the results of the Uruguay Round, which reach far beyond the old General Agreement of Tariffs and Trade (GATT). Besides the traditional GATT remit of overseeing trade in goods, the results of the eighth round of GATT talks encompass among other things rules on trade in services, protecting intellectual property, and wider institutional competences in settling trade disputes. Furthermore, GATT's old no-go areas such as trade in agro-products textiles and clothing, were integrated in its body of rules.

The role and participation of developing countries underwent considerable changes during the course of the new Uruguay Round. Before the talks began, many governments of the south took a highly critical stance on the taking up of the negotiations, and above all on the widening of their brief. Leading critics among the developing countries, such as Brazil and India, called for the effective implementation of the results of the Tokyo round (1973-79) before beginning new talks. This thumbs-down gave a glimpse once again of the unity of developing countries, which during the 1970s set the trade policy agenda and contributed to the flourishing of the UN Conference on Trade and Development (UNCTAD). But their increasing differences in economic interests were soon reflected in disparate negotiating positions during the GATT talks. In some sectors such as agricultural trade, the developing countries no longer had any common interests whatsoever. Nevertheless, both during and after the round there were various attempts to assess the possible impacts of trade liberalisation on the developing countries as a whole. The World Bank and the OECD's Development Assistance Committee tried very early in the negotiations to make the possible results palatable for the developing countries with encouraging projections. The developing countries' high rate of accession to the WTO reflects the growing importance of the world trade order for them. And many of them are meanwhile pushing ahead with liberalisation of their own economies, partly of their own accord and partly in the context of structural adjustment programmes. But they often evaluate the results of the Uruguay Round quite differently. The following is aimed at summarizing briefly the possible political and economic impacts of the developing countries, which have been the subject of debate so far.

Stricter Rules on World Trade

The Uruguay Round led to a widening and strengthening of the body of rules on world trade. Its widening covered the inclusion of the above-mentioned new sectors and the old areas of exception. Its strengthening relates to the drawing up of stricter rules for fixing standards to counter the growing use of non-tariff obstacles to trade, and to the new procedure for settling disputes. While under the old rules all treaty states had to approve the ruling of an arbitration procedure—including the "loser" country—to make it valid, an arbitration now takes effect directly. Only its unanimous rejection by the treaty signatories can make it null and void.

NGOs in the North and the South in particular interpret both the widening and strengthening critically. In their view, the changes give the WTO too much power. They fear that national political decisions in future could be assessed and attacked as possible trade obstacles. They say this reduces the already limited possibilities of nation states to determine important policy fields, such as the environment and social or regional policy.

Strong and Weak Members

However, to what extent these legal remedies can actually be resorted to in the everyday life of global trade policy remains to be seen in the near future. As early as during US ratification of the Uruguay Round, the Clinton Administration commented that if USA were to be censured three times by a GATT dispute process it would reserve the right to leave the organisation again. Since weaker trade partners lack the possibility to take pain-inflicting countermeasures, the different trade policy weights of the WTO members will also count in future practice.

The estimates of individual groups of developing countries on possible economic profits stemming from Uruguay Round differ greatly. Projections of potential trade profits were downright euphoric even before the end of the negotiations.

The general reduction of custom duties on industrial goods-put about 37 per cent—will impact on the developing countries as a whole because the previous preferential tariffs will become relatively less important. There will be few changes for countries that have so far hardly taken advantage of preferences. But the cutback will impact in particular on African countries, which have the most extensive preferences, as well as on the ASEAN group, which were especially high users of the Generalized System of Preferences. A loss of 1.5 per cent is projected for Sub-Saharan Africa and the ACP states, and 1.9 per cent for LDC's. According to Overseas Development Institute (ODI) estimates, the figures for individual countries could be much worse. Ethiopia, Malawi, Mozambique and Guayana are likely to lose between 4.6 per cent and 5.9 per cent of their export earings.

Agricultural Markets Remain Distorted

In the agricultural sector, the net food importers among the developing countries will be losers because they will have to pay moderately higher prices for their imports. The forecasts of losses, however, are not so high since no far-reaching liberalisation can be achieved in the agro-sector. The two main adversaries in Uruguay Round's dispute over agriculture, the USA and the EU, were able in the Blair House Agreement to reach an accord on only a very limited reduction of their high support payments to their farmers. Even cutbacks in export subsidies were pegged at about only 21 per cent in volume and about 36 per cent in value. That is why export subsidies will continue to exert pressure on world market prices. At the same time, the slight reduction will mean the net agricultural produce exporters among the developing countries will derive only marginal profit from the liberalisation.

On the positive side, the most important sector of projected profits for developing countries is textiles and clothing. The accord on these goods foresees the previous Multifibre Agreement (MFA) expiring within 10 years and textiles and clothing coming step-by-step under GATT rules. But is remains to be seen if that target can be achieved in that period, and how often in future the industrial countries will invoke the protective clause covering this sector to safeguard their own industries.

Weak States will Lose

Taking an overall look at the results of the Uruguay Round, it can be noted that those developing countries, which are strong in exports of industrial goods and have so far hardly used the Generalized System of Preference, will profit economically. The losers will be countries, which will suffer from the erosion of the importance of preferences. Totting up, negative impacts of more than US $ 2 billion are forecast for Africa. Various sides—NGOs as well as some governments-are therefore now calling for compensation payments for net losers.

The developing countries lost unity came to life again towards the end of the Uruguay Round when new subjects for world trade order were put on the agenda. Some governments and NGOs are increasingly addressing the ecological and social impacts of the liberalisation of world trade. There are above all highly vocal in expressing fears that the globalisation of the world economy will be accompanied by a loss of national sovereignty over political measures in sectors such as the environment and social and regional policy. And that linked with an increasingly competitive situation in an ever more open world market. This will in the long-term have negative impacts on a country's ability to assert justified measures to protect its interests. The governments of most developing countries have clearly rejected these new proposals for discussion. They fear this bid could make the industrial nations' hopes for economic protectionism reappear.

New Role for WTO

There is no simple answer to these new agendas. Indeed, it is questionable if the WTO is a suitable forum to negotiate on them in detail. However, so long as a relatively effective government body on world trade relations has no counterpart in comparably effective instruments to deal with the social and ecological impacts of globalisation, there will probably be repeated attempts to assign new competencies to the WTO. Even when it would make more sense not to leave multilateral rules on environmental protection or securing human rights to a trade organisation. That nothing should block the objectives of sustainable development or safeguarding human rights, which go beyond trade policy, must thereby be beyond doubt.

24

Income Gap Widens

The gap in income among the people of the world has been widening. In 1960, according to United Nations statisticians, the richest 20 per cent of the world's people received 30 times more income than the poorest 20 per cent. By 1991, they were getting 61 times more. While the poorest one-fifth in 1960 received a meagre 2.3 per cent of world income, by 1991 that revenue share had fallen to 1.4 per cent. The income share of the richest fifth, meanwhile, rose from 70 per cent to 85 per cent.

These disparities prevail both among countries and within them, and the large gap between individuals world wide reflects the combination of both of those splits. Almost four fifths of all people live in the developing world, where incomes are only fraction of those in industrial countries. In turn, within countries in both categories, gaps in income between citizens can be even wider.

The widest income gap reported within a country is in Botswana, where during the 1980s the richest 20 per cent of society received over 47 times more income than the poorest 20 per cent. Brazil was second, with a ratio of 32 to 1. In Guatemala and Panama, the ratio stood at 30 to 1.

The rapidly growing economies of East Asia have had income patterns similar to those of Western Europe and North America, with the richest one-fifth often earning 5 to 10 times more than the poorest fifth. In South Asia, India, Bangladesh, and Pakistan have had relatively even distributions of income, with the richest 20 per cent getting only four to five times more than the poorest quintile. Some countries that have had military conflicts apparently based in part on inequities among citizens, never the less have relatively even income distributions.

The split between countries and people can be seen in the marketplace. The value of luxury goods sales world-wide—high-fashion clothing and top-of-the-line autos, for example-exceeds the gross national products of two-thirds of the worlds countries. The world's average income, roughly $4,000 a year, is well below the US poverty line.

The poorest fifth of the world accounted for 0.9 per cent of world trade, 1.1 per cent of global domestic investment, 0.9 per cent of global domestic savings, and just 0.2 per cent of global commercial credit at the beginning of the 1990s. Each of those shares declined between 1960 and 1990.

These disparities are reflected in the consumption of many resources. At the start of this decade, industrial countries home to roughly a fifth of the world's population, accounted for about 86 per cent of the consumption of aluminium, and chemicals, 81 per cent of the paper, 80 per cent of the iron and steel, and three-quarters of the timber and energy. Since then, economic growth in developing countries has probably reduced these percentages. China's economy, for example, is more than 50 per cent larger now than it was in 1990, and developing countries have passed industrial ones in fertilizer consumption.

Uneven income distribution is shaping some of the most important trends in the world today. It raises crime rates, for example. And it drives migration. People have long responded to economic disparities by following a path from poor regions to richer ones, as tens of millions of workers chase higher wages and better opportunities. Some 1.6 million Asians and Middle Easterners were working in Kuwait and Saudi Arabia before they fled war in 1991, and at least 2.5 million Mexicans live in the United States.

The same is true within countries: rising disparities of income are adding to the growth of cities thorough rural to urban migration. Latin America, with some of the highest disparities of income among its citizens, is also the most urbanized region of the developing world—not entirely by coincidence. Since 1950, city dwellers there have risen from 42 per cent of the population to 73 per cent.

For many years, china had one of the most equal distributions of income in the world. But now that is changing, as incomes in its southern provinces and special economic zones soar while those in rural areas rise much more slowly. Also not coincidentally, the Chinese National Academy of Social Sciences forecasts that by 2010, half the population will live in cities, compared with 28 per cent today and only 10 per cent in the early 1980s.

In the early 1990s, developing world economies, especially, in East Asia, have grown faster than the economies of the industrial countries. This has the potential to shrink disparities of income, if poorer countries continue to catch up. Yet even if the gaps among countries narrow, the gaps between people may not, because economic growth is distributed so unevenly within nations. Despite the recent restoration of economic growth in Latin America, no progress is expected in reducing poverty, which is even likely to increase slightly.

Meanwhile, in some regions almost no one has been getting richer. The per capita income of most sub Saharan African nations actually fell during the 1980's. In sub-Saharan Africa, the poorest geographic region, an estimated one-third of all college graduates have left the continent. That loss of talented people, due in large part to poverty and a lack of opportunities in Africa, will make it even more difficult for the continent to advance.

The economic growth that has the potential to close income gaps among peoples in the developing world is instead becoming a splitting off, with some parts of societies joining the industrial world while others remain behind. Singapore, Hongkong, and Taiwan have begun to look like wealthy industrial countries, for example. Now parts of China are following, as are the wealthier segments of Latin American society and of Southeast Asian countries. This is good news for members of the middle-income countries and for the world. But it may do little to help the poorest fifth of humanity.

25

A New World Order for Whom?

"Four holocausts" humanity has produced are breeding the seeds of our own destruction: war and militarisation, human oppression, economic destitution and environmental destruction. The "new world orders" on offer can satisfy only the minority of the world's rich and will ultimately only exacerbate these four trends towards global annihilation. But there is also hope in the "grassroots world order" leading to the civil society, democratisation and social mobilisation as the only way for the planet to survive.

As we approach the end of the 20th century and a new millennium, humanity is faced with four conditions of its own making, so serious in terms of their present destruction of life and risks for the future that they warrant a description as "four holocausts".

The first holocaust is that of war and militarisation. After the Gulf War it is clear that, far from preparing the way for world peace, that conflict has unleashed a new global arms race in the weapons whose brutal effectiveness was so clearly demonstrated in Iraq. The second holocaust is that of human oppression, the violent denial by governments of the basic personal, civil, political and economic rights of their citizens, which routinely persist in a majority of countries of the world. The third holocaust is that of economic destitution, the mass poverty of a fifth of the world's population, leading to endemic malnutrition, disease and death, not least among children. And the fourth holocaust is that of environmental destruction, which is gradually or not so gradually rendering the planet uninhabitable, as witnessed by the growing millions of environmental refugees whose bankrupt ecosystems can no longer support them.

None of these circumstances is entirely new to our age, of course, War, repression, destitution and ecological degradation have often been part of the human condition. What is new about the current situation is its global nature. All humanity, the whole earth, is now at risk. And it is all humanity which must be party to a response, if it is to be successful.

Against this threatening background, several new developments stand out. First, is the collapse of communism, taking out of the bounds of credibility socialism's millenarian dream of abolishing the market and inevitably replacing capitalism through the onward march of history. Second, there are the twin trends of globalisation and interdependence: globalisation especially of the economy, interdependence especially through environmental impacts. This is the context for any discussion of a "new world order".

The New World Orders

There are, broadly, three kinds of new world orders currently on offer. The real world is almost certainly going to be mixture of all three, but the balance between them will be crucial in deciding whether we will successfully manage to face, and overcome, the holocausts raging among us.

The first kind of new world order may be called the "neoliberal". Its most important component is the untrammelled operation of what we would call the global "free market". At once we must qualify this terminology by noting that the freedom bestowed on someone by the market is in direct proportion to the amount of property owned by that person within it. In a free market, those who own the means of production are free to produce what, when and where they want, and largely to determine the conditions of production. Those who own the means of consumption can similarly scour the world for products to satisfy their wants. The extent to which this "freedom" is far from universal is shown by the fact that, with regard to consumption some 23 per cent of the world's population control 85 per cent of the income which is consumptions prerequisite and ownership of the means of production is more concentrated still. The neoliberal world order thus represents a good deal for perhaps a quarter of the world's population, but has precious little to offer the rest.

A Global Order Framed by International Institutions

The second kind of new world order may be termed the "social democratic" and is roughly that advocated in the 1970's by the proponents of a New International Economic Order. These two new world orders clearly different but they also share several characteristics which seem to be more significant than their differences. First, they are explicitly western-oriented and homogenizing. They view the world through the eyes of western science and western culture simultaneously devaluing the knowledge and accumulated wisdom of the great majority of human kind. The paradigm society, towards which all others are supposed to be developing or aspiring to develop, is that of the United States.

Second, both these world orders are economistic. Human progress and development to them means economic developments, still usually measured by the level and growth of GNP per person. No social or cultural tradition or aspiration is allowed to stand in the way of this "development". Third, both world views envisage top-down decision-making for administration and control. For the neoliberals the dominant influence is exercised by the owners and managers of transnational capital. For the social democrats their influence is balanced by the interventions of international and national bureaucrats. Neither world order places great store on consultation with, let alone decision-making by, ordinary people in their communities.

In contrast to these two new world orders, it is possible to posit a third, here called the grassroots new world order, which takes as its principal focus neither the market nor the state (national or international), but civil society, the networks of family, community and voluntary association acting for social reproduction, reconstruction or reform. This new world order has characteristics diametrically opposed to those shared by the first two discussed. Its impulse derives explicity from the bottom up, drawing on the capability and creativity of those united by shared values and interests, at the local level or in wider networks. Their world-view is one of cultural diversity, of one world comprised of many different villages rather than a homogeneous global village modelled on the US. They perceive human development to be holistic, with the economic dimension integrated with, or embedded in, a broader social, ethical and ecological reality. And they proceed from an ethical basis that strives for ecological sustainability, social justice in distribution and broad participation is cultural, political and economic life.

Looking to the Grassroots World Order

After this thumbnail sketch of these three views of different dominant global processes, one can ask which of them or, more realistically, what balance between them, will be best able to put an end to the four holocausts tormenting humanity. There is only one convincing answer: the dominant thrust must be towards the grassroots new world order. There are several reasons for this. Most obviously, it is indisputable that it is the forces of the market and the state that have not only failed to douse, but have actually fanned the flames of all four holocausts. It is states that go to war and waste the commonwealth on weaponry. It is states that are responsible for the great majority of violence and repression against ordinary people. It is states, often supported by multilateral governmental organisations such as the World Bank and IMF, that have the so called Third World intervened massively in the subsistence, largely nonmarket economies of the people, and redistributed their resources, redefining their very rights to property, in favour of industrialisation and market exchange. But these enhanced markets have then spectacularly failed to provide alternative subsistence for those dispossessed, leaving them by the million impoverished, marginalized and destitute. Moreover, this process has set in train two great engines of environmental destruction: industrialisation itself, with its toxic pollution, soil erosion, water and ozone depletion and climate destabilisation; and the depredations of the rural dispossessed, forced into forests or onto marginal lands, deforesting, making deserts, extinguishing species and multiplying in numbers in their desperate efforts to stay alive.

Civil Society Mobilizing for Human Survival

In contrast, it is civil society that has mobilized explicitly against the four holocausts. The great social movements of our time are those for peace and human rights, for justice and development, and for environmental conservation. It is independent, non-violent associations of civil society that have sought explicitly to address these issues, meeting at best indifference from organisations of the market and the state, at worst outright hostility.

This is not at all to say that the market and state are irredeemable, or that they have no role in combating the four holocausts of destruction. On the contrary, they each have a vital contribution to make but, it order to make it, each must first be transformed. The market failures caused by great concentrations of wealth and power, ubiquitous externalities, the tyranny of small decisions and positional goods can only be resolved by determined and democratic state action. But most governments are not democratic. On the contrary most are unrepresentative and self-serving, many are vicious and corrupt. And the only force that can democratize them is that of civil mobilisation and organisation.

Viewing the immense power of today's concentrations of wealth, and the remoteness of most governments from their people, one may feel despair at the prospect of civil society being able to harness these forces to the common good. And indeed there is no certainty that they will be thus harnessed. The four holocausts may simply run their awful course. But since 1989, at least, there is proof positive in the peaceful revolutions in Eastern Europe and the Soviet Union, that civil society can overturn seemingly omnipotent despotic structures. And all over the world the various movements for peace, justice and the environment are organizing for human survival. The stakes have never been so high and the outcome is uncertain; but there are legitimate, and inspiring, grounds for hope.

26

Beyond the Uruguay Round:

Opportunities and Challenges

The successful conclusion of the Uruguay Round was the most significant economic event of 1994. The Round contributed to liberalisation of trade in goods, services and investment. It represents a decisive step towards introducing market solutions in international transactions. It entails significant potential gains for the world economy. But the distribution of gains across regions, nations and various groups within countries will be uneven. Giving rise to certain challenges and risks. These merit the attention of the international community.

The process of trade liberalisation intensifies the trend towards globalisation. Free movements of goods and services across countries will mean greater mobility of capital and foreign direct investment. These factors taken together should contribute to the efficiency of the world economy by encouraging countries to produce goods and services in which they hold a comparative advantage. International competition on price and quality will thus intensify, leading to the development of new products and processes.

The downside of this process is however, that it can accelerate two other trends. The first is the concentration of market structures, both at the global and national levels. The role of transnational corporations in the world economy is increasing, and while much stress is justifiably laid on promoting small and medium sized enterprises, there is no doubt that big business will have a growing role in economic activities not only in developed but also in developing countries. Even if measures are taken to prevent, through competition policy, possible abuses of dominant positions by large enterprises, the trend towards concentration of market power through globalisation will continue to have important implications for world trade and production.

The second trend is towards the potential margainalisation of poor nations and vulnerable groups within nations. The least developed countries, particularly in sub-Saharan Africa, for example, will experience losses in the short and even medium term as a result of the Uruguay Round agreements. They lack sufficient supply capacity to produce and export goods for which market access has improved. More importantly, they will not be able to exercise policy options that were available to the newly industrialized countries during their early development stage. Further, their competitive position in the world economy might be weakened with the new trends towards regionalism, as well as new methods of production.

Conversely, the intensification of international competition will inevitably enhance the position of the most efficient producers, with implications for the location of industries, and hence for employment. This will add fuel to the arguments of the advocates of protectionism.

Therefore, although the world economy as a whole benefits from trade liberalisation, there are risks of marginalisation which may lead to tensions among nations and among various groups within them and eventually could result in trade conflicts, undermining the security of the international trading system. The threat of instability of the trading system arises, in a sense, from a sort of "prisoners dilemma"

Whereby the common interest of the universe as a whole may diverge from the perceived individual interests of the main participating countries. Countries have a common interest in liberalizing international trade. However, individual countries may feel their interest lies in restricting trade so as to, inter alia, "protect" jobs. The balance could then be tipped in favour of protectionism, either overt or disguised as anti-dumping measures or environmental criteria and health and labour standards applied unilaterally. Likewise, the argument for the protection of strategic industries may be invoked.

As the invisible hand of the market by itself is insufficient to bring about social justice at the national level, market forces alone are equally incapable of preserving the common interest of all nations in a globalized world economy. A liberalized global economy requires a suitable framework of governance and institutions. In particular, like the need for a social safety net at the national level to avert social conflicts, there is also a need for a safety net at the international level to prevent the weakening of the international trading system, the environmental commons and peaceful international relations. Our existing institutional set-ups tend to lag behind economic changes, both at the national and international levels.

At the national level there is need for strengthening the social mechanisms and to pay closer attention to the distributional aspects of the benefits of production and trade; this is also true at the international level. Furthermore, there is a need for strengthening the socioeconomic functions in order to find pragmatic solutions to universal problems arising from change and to preserve the common interests of people everywhere. Sound analysis is called for in this regard. A creative approach is needed, departing as necessary from conventional views and aimed at arriving at commitments implementable by all.

27

The WTO Dispute Settlement Mechanism

The Uruguay Round's new dispute settlement mechanism represents the new teeth of the Wold Trade Organisation (WTO). "The dispute settlement system of the WTO is a central element in providing security and predictability to the multilateral trading system", states the Understanding on Rules and Procedures Governing the Settlement of Disputes.

In the Final Act, WTO members have committed themselves not to take unilateral action against perceived violations of the trade rules. Instead, they have pledged to seek recourse in the new dispute-settlement system, and abide by its rules and procedures.

The Understanding emphasizes that prompt settlement of disputes is essential to the effective functioning of the WTO. Thus, it sets out in great detail the procedures and the timetable to be followed in resolving disputes—pin contrast with the current GATT whose dispute-settlement provisions are contained in just low Articles. The existing GATT procedures have been built up over time through the evolution of customary practice, and later codified in decisions by GATT contracting parties—notably the 1979 Understanding and a provisional streamlining of the system in the 1989 Improvements following the Mid-Term Review of the Round.

Under the WTO, there will be one *Dispute Settlement Body(DSB)* dealing with dispute arising from any agreement contained in the Final Act. Thus, the DSB will have the sole authority to establish panels, adopt panel and appellate reports, maintain surveillance of implementation of rulings and recommendations, and authorize retaliatory measures in cases of non-implementation of recommendations. This is a significant improvement over the current GATT, under which dispute settlement is fragmented between the Council and the various Tokyo Round Committees.

Other important new features distinguish the WTO mechanism from that of GATT. In the WTO, there has to be a consensus against the establishment of panels or adoption of panel reports for these decisions not to be made whereas the reverse is true for the current system. Thus, parties to the dispute in the new system can no longer block these decisions. Another new feature is the possibility of appealing panel decisions to a standing Appellate Body. And, in line with the new integrated nature of the WTO mechanism, complainants, as a last resort, may take retaliatory action—suspend concessions—under an agreement different form the one covering the dispute against a member that has not implemented adopted panel recommendations.

The following are the various stages involved in setting disputes in the WTO:

Consultations

The aim of the WTO dispute-settlement mechanism is "to secure a positive solution to a dispute". Thus, developing a mutually acceptable solution consistent with WTO provisions to a problem between members is encouraged throughout the dispute-settlement process.

The first stage of settling disputes is the holding of consultations between the members concerned. Any member should reply promptly (within 10 days) to a request for consultations, and enter into consultations within 30 days from the date of the request. To ensure transparency, any request for consultations should be notified to the DSB in writing, providing the reasons for the request, including identification of the measure at issue and the legal basis for the complaint.

If consultations fail, and if both parties so agree, the case at this stage can be brought to the WTO Director-General, who, acting in an ex-officio capacity. Will be ready to offer good offices, conciliation or mediation to settle the dispute.

Establishment of Panels

If the member concerned do not respond to a request for consultations within10 days or if the consultations fail to arrive at a solution after 60 days, the complainant can ask the DSB to establish a panel to examine the case.

The establishment of a panel is almost automatic. The procedures require that the DSB should establish a panel no later than the second time it considers the panel request, unless there is a consensus against the decision. This means that the government which is the subject of the complaint cannot block the establishment of the panel.

The determination of the panel's terms of reference as well as its composition is also straightforward. The Understanding provides for standard terms of reference that mandate the panel to examine the complaint in the light of the agreement cited, and to make findings that will assist the DSB in making recommendations or in giving rulings provided for in that agreement. The panel may operate under different terms of reference, if the parties concerned so agree.

The panel is to be constituted within 30 days of its establishment. The WTO Secretariat will suggest the names of three potential panelists to the parties to the dispute , drawing as necessary on a list of qualified persons (including, for example, those who have previously participated in panel proceedings, or have been representatives to GATT, or have taught international trade law). If the parties cannot agree on the panelists within 20 days form the establishment of the panel, at the request of either party, the Director General, in consultations with the DSB Chairman and the Chairman of the relevant Committee or Council, will appoint the panelists. The panelists will serve in their individual capacities and will not be subjects to government instructions.

Panel Procedures

The understanding provides that the period in which the panel conducts its examination of the case—that is, from the time the terms of reference and composition of the panel are agreed to the time the panel's final report is given to the parties to the dispute—should not exceed six months. In cases of urgency, those relating to perishable goods, the timeframe is shortened to three months. In no case should the period from the establishment of the panel to the circulation of the report to the Members exceed nine months.

Detailed working procedures for the panel are set out in the Understanding (see chart).

Adoption of Panel Reports

The WTO procedures provide that a panel report is to be adopted by the DSB within 60 days of issuance, unless one party notifies its decision to appeal or a consensus emerges against the adoption of the report.

The DSB cannot consider the adoption of a panel report earlier than 20 days after it has been circulated to members. Members which have objections to the report are required to state their reasons in writing, for circulation before the DSB meeting at which the panel report will be considered.

Appellate Review

A new feature of the WTO dispute settlement mechanism gives the possibility of appeal to either party in a panel proceeding. However, any appeal shall be limited to issues of law covered in the panel report and the legal interpretation developed by the panel.

All appeals will be heard by a standing Appellate Body to be established by the DSB. This Appellate Body will be compose of seven persons—broadly representative of the WTO membership—who will serve four-year terms. They are to be persons of recognized standing in the field of law and international trade, and not affiliated with any government.

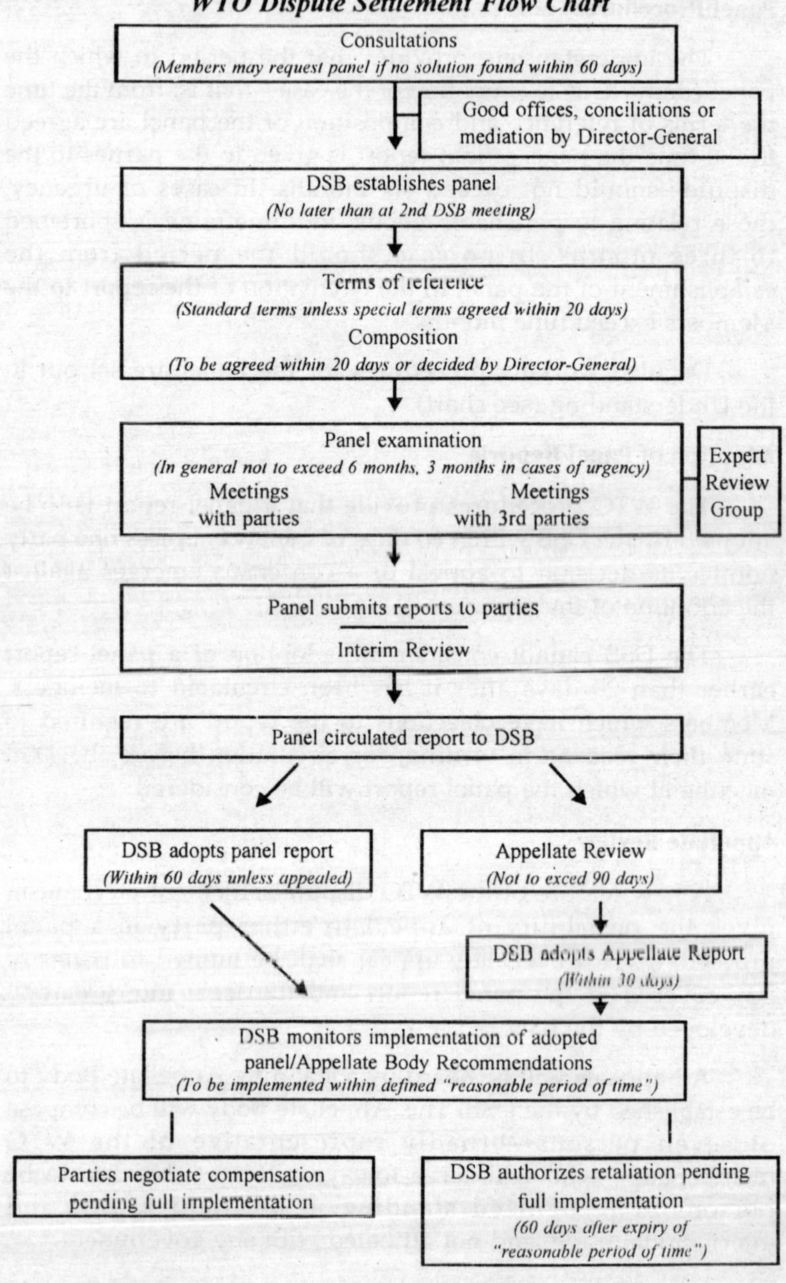

WTO Dispute Settlement Flow Chart
Consultations
(Members may request panel if no solution found within 60 days)
Good offices, conciliations or mediation by Director-General
DSB establishes panel
(No later than at 2nd DSB meeting)
Terms of reference
(Standard terms unless special terms agreed within 20 days)
Composition
(To be agreed within 20 days or decided by Director-General)
Panel examination
(In general not to exceed 6 months, 3 months in cases of urgency)
Meetings with parties
Meetings with 3rd parties
Expert Review Group
Panel submits reports to parties
Interim Review
Panel circulated report to DSB
DSB adopts panel report
(Within 60 days unless appealed)
Appellate Review
(Not to exced 90 days)
DSB adopts Appellate Report
(Within 30 days)
DSB monitors implementation of adopted panel/Appellate Body Recommendations
(To be implemented within defined "reasonable period of time")
Parties negotiate compensation pending full implementation
DSB authorizes retaliation pending full implementation
(60 days after expiry of "reasonable period of time")

Three members of the Appellate Body sit at any one time to hear appeals. They can uphold, modify or reverse the legal findings and conclusions of the panel. As a general rule, the appeal proceedings are not to exceed 60 days but in no case shall they exceed 90 days.

Thirty days after issuance, the Appellate Body report is to be adopted by the DSB and unconditionally accepted by the parties to the dispute-unless there is consensus against its adoption.

Implementation

The Understanding stresses that "prompt compliance with recommendations or rulings of the DSB is essential in order to ensure effective resolution of disputes to the benefit of all Members."

At a DSB meeting held within 30 days of the adoption of the panel or appellate report, the party concerned must state its intentions in respect of the implementation of the recommendations. If it is impractical to comply immediately, the member will be given a "reasonable period of time"—to be set by the DSB—to do so. If it fails to act within this period, it is obliged to enter into negotiations with the complainant in order to determine a mutually acceptable compensation.

If after 20 days, no satisfactory compensation is agreed, the complainant may request authorisation from the DSB to suspend concessions or obligations against the other party. The procedures provide that the DSB should grant this authorisation within 30 days of the expiry of the "reasonable period of time" unless there is a consensus against the request.

If the member concerned objects to the level of suspension, the matter will be referred to arbitration. This will be carried out by the original panel members, and if this is not possible, by an arbitrator appointed by the WTO Director General. Arbitration should be completed within 60 days of the expiry of the "reasonable period of time", and the resulting decision should be accepted by the parties concerned as final and not subject to another arbitration. The DSB, upon request, then authorizes the suspension of concessions consistent with the findings of the arbitrator, unless there is a consensus to reject the request.

In principle, concessions should be suspended in the same sector as that in issue in the panel case. If this is not practicable or effective, the suspension can be made in a different sector of the same agreement. In turn, if this is not effective or practicable and if the circumstances are serious enough, the suspension of concessions may be made under another agreement.

In any case, the DSB will keep under surveillance the implementation of adopted recommendations or rulings, and any outstanding case will remain on its agenda until the issue is resolved.

28

New Agenda of the WTO

One "new" issue that is already in the WTO work programme is the relationship between trade and the environment. At the heart of the matter is how to relate the rules-based multilateral trade system, continued trade liberalisation and further development of the global economy to environmental concerns and objectives. It is possible to envisage circumstances, in which trade, unsupported by sound environmental policy, could involve damage to the environment—or, on the contrary, in which environmental regulations could harm legitimate trade. In such circumstances, however, careful judgment is necessary in weighing whether it is trade policy or environmental policy which must be adjusted, it is also not difficult to see how ill-considered international environmental agreement could needlessly frustrate trade and reduce incomes and even put risk environmental reform and improvement. At the same time, it is just as important to recognize the circumstances in which, by encouraging efficiency and a better allocation of scarce resources, trade liberalisation may be supportive of an improved environment. The WTO will contribute to a better understanding of the issues, and assist governments in developing more coherent polices in this area.

Trade and investment is leading candidate for the new agenda, since one of the consequences of globalisation is to lessen the distinctions among different forms of market access. In the GATT framework, market access simply in terms of tariffs and non-tariff measures. Reducing tariffs and eliminating other trade barrier at the frontier was the recipe for liberalisation. Foreign investment was an altogether different matter, Indeed, countries often used to regard tariffs and other trade barriers as convenient mechanisms for inducing foreign investment. Protection of the domestic market offered attractive profits to foreign investors. This was the essence of the import substitution development strategy—a strategy that in large measure failed and has now been discredited. In today's world of international business, trade and investment are increasingly viewed as complements, not substitutes. Different parts of internationally based businesses can be located in several different countries. Increasingly, businesses trade to invest, and invest to trade. The WTO cannot afford to concern itself only with the trade side of the equation—that would be to deny the reality of modern global business practices.

It is not coincidence that foreign direct investment flows worldwide quadrupled, to almost US $ 200 billion per annum, in the ten year to 1993. Indeed, the importance of investment was recognized in the General Agreement on Trade in Services negotiated in the Uruguay Round, where investment, or commercial presence, was one of the four modes of service supply in respect of which WTO members undertook market access commitments. But there is a need for a broader or more horizontal approach to international investment rules. Such rules would build on the WTO principles of non-discrimination and national treatment, and create a policy environment to encourage and safeguard foreign investment, whether in goods or services.

Governments will increasingly recognize the need for work on investment in a more global setting as well. Especially so since developing countries are not only the target of a growing proportion of international investment but are themselves becoming important overseas investors. One should note that the Uruguay Round Agreement on Trade-Related Investment Measures calls for an examination by members within five years of the case for developing provisions on investment policy.

That same mandate refers to competition policy, which also has to be examined as a possible candidate for further work, Of course, what has done in the GATT and the WTO over 50 years in promoting a liberal trading environment is precisely the enhancement of competition. But if we have succeeded in getting the rules of competition between countries to work effectively, that very success requires us to go further and consider how the behaviour of companies can serve to distort international competition. The need to see whether there are any areas where explicit competition rules, or specific understandings, are necessary internationally to complement the statutes that many governments already have on their books. There is no doubt that competition rules are essential to the proper functioning of markets-the need to clarify, however, is how best to promote such disciplines, both nationally and internationally.

Trade and social standards. This is a highly controversial issue, and in the absence of a consensus there is no possibility that it could be brought into the agenda of the WTO. It is clear that what the need first and foremost is a comprehensive effort to bring some clarity to the many complex issues that are involved here.

The first issue to be clarified is the nature of the subject; talking about the comparative advantage of developing countries which comes from lower wage level—as the issue is sometimes presented or talking about human rights or labour standard? It is fundamentally important to clarify the terms of the debate as it relates to trade. The second point is to identify what are the key issues related to trade; for example, talking about child labour or trade union rights in terms of labour standards or in terms of human rights? There are just some of the preconditions for opening a discussion on whether a useful debate is in fact possible on these issues. One of these principles is that economic and social growth and development are to a large extent interdependent. When the economic situation is poor the social situation is also likely to be poor. And correspondingly, where there is economic growth, social development is more likely to come too.

While no-one should challenge the legitimate right of developing countries to use the comparative advantage of lower costs, and no-one should use human rights and issues of social standards as an excuse for disguised protectionism, no country should deliberately deny workers' rights or attempt to generate artificially-lower costs by forced labour, discrimination against women, exploitation of children or other such abuses.

No one should on no account allow this debate to re-open a North-South divide. Dialogue is the best approach to fining ways to improve the observance of labour standards. In order to convince developing countries that no projectionist considerations are involved in the debate, it is essential to prove that all possible measures other than trade sanctions are being taken to alleviate the problems. One excellent example is the Memorandum of Understanding on the elimination of child labour from the garments industry in Bangladesh that was signed in July 1995 by the industry, the ILO and UNICEF, with support from the Bangladesh an US Governments. This joint approach combines restrictions on child labour with the improvement of educational opportunities for the children involved. This is a targeted and constructive approach to a specific problem, and as such it offers a useful model for future efforts. On the other hand, to simply restrict imports of garments from the industries concerned would in all likelihood have just worsened the situation of these children.

Reciprocity and Regionalism

Reciprocity and the growth of regionalism in international trade relations is very important. There are from to time calls for trade policies based on reciprocity instead of the basic Most Favoured Nations (MFN) principle. These are based on the assumption that the degree of liberalisation already reached by certain countries does not give them any real defence in a multilateral negotiation vis à vis those countries whose liberalisation process is much less advanced. Advocates of reciprocity argue that such countries have no real incentive to deeper liberalisation, given their benefits from the MFN system.

To present reciprocity as an alternative to MFN is a major departure from the trading system built up over 50 years, and it is just the opposite of what the founding fathers of the multilateral system envisaged. A nation or regional group which believes itself to be an open market has the right to fight hard to obtain from all its partners the greatest possible degree of liberalisation. If this argument is used tactically and temporarily as a negotiating device, there is less need for alarm over its implications for the system as a whole. But if alarm over its implications for the system as whole. But if it becomes a permanent instrument of policy, then the risk for the multilateral system could become serious.

Trade is technical in its substance but highly political in its consequences. Reciprocity as a structural alternative to the multilateral system equals bilateralism; bilateralism equals discrimination; and trade relations based on power rather than rules are the result. This would be a very dangerous departure from the success story of the multilateral system.

The growth of regionalism is a more complex issue. There is no natural contradiction between regionalism and the multilateral system. This has been the shared assessment of the great majority of the international trade community. The real contradiction, it must always be emphasized, is between open trade and protectionism. Regional trade initiatives can certainly help to lower trade barriers and thus promote economic growth. But the relationship between regionalism and a multilateral system based on the MFN principle is nonetheless a complex one. The provisions of the GATT have sought to ensure compatibility by requiring regional agreements to cover substantially all trade among the partners and to promoted trade policies which do no lead to higher protection or extra restrictions on the trade of non-members. In practice however, it has been almost impossible to assess the consistency of regional agreements.

The relation between regional and multilateral liberalisation in practice has been a different and generally more positive story. For example, successive enlargements of the European Union have been followed by multilateral trade negotiations, which have maintained a *de facto* link between progress at the regional level and at the multilateral level. These links are the reason why most people have seen regional agreements as building blocks for multilateral free trade.

Until quite recently, there was only one large regional grouping, and that was limited to a number of western European countries. The US was historically opposed to regionalism. But this situation has changed, since the 1980s, the US has begun to build its own regional agreements, though free trade with Canada, through NAFTA, and through APEC, etc. Now, almost all the member countries of the WTO also belong to a regional trade agreement. The importance of regional agreements as a means of tariff reduction has declined (this is also thanks to the success of the GATT). Regional agreements are becoming more and more important in terms of trade rules and for the political weight they represent in international negotiations. These are elements, which could break up the parallelism between regional and multilateral progress; there is the risk that antagonism between regional groups could make progress in the multilateral system more difficult.

Furthermore, regional initiatives such as the suggestions for a trans-Atlantic free trade area could give the impression of re-erecting a discriminatory divide between the rich North and the poorer South. One must be very attentive to strengthening the linkage, which has existed up to now between regional and multilateral progress. What this means in practical terms is that regional liberalisation initiatives must proceed almost in tandem with multilateral ones. What countries are willing to do regionally, they must then be willing to do multilaterally, so as to keep this parallelism between regional and multilateral commitments.

At the core of this relationship, there is the basic question of the kind of international system, that is needed a global system based on the principle of non-discrimination embodied in agreed and enforceable rules, or a world divided into regional blocs with all the consequences this would imply for political stability and security.

An Unusual Historic Opportunity

To sum up, it is clear that the challenges facing the multilateral trading system are about much more than trade matters as they used to be defined. For some people—and for some countries too—the pace of change is unsettling and even alarming. Whether in the challenges that the information revolution presents to anyone over 30, or in the pace of economic globalisation, there is an understandable reflex which asks the world to slow down a little. However, we know will not.

That is why there is a need to keep the multilateral system, with its reliable framework of principles and rules in good repair, it is a firm foothold in a shifting world. Liberalisation within the multilateral system means that this unstoppable process can be implemented within internationally agreed rules and disciplines. This is the opposite of a chaotic and unchecked process—without the security of the multilateral system, change would indeed be a leap in the dark.

At the same time, the multilateral system is becoming more and more a political issue. This is happening because its evolution increasingly concerns national regulatory policies more than cross-border obstacles, and it is happening because the challenges to the system are increasingly political rather than technical. In this context, it could become very important to consider the possibility of strengthening the institutional basis of the system—for example by enhancing the political dimension of its central institution, the WTO.

The confluence of political and economic events of the last few years places everyone on the threshold of an unusual historic opportunity: that of establishing a truly global system for the conduct of international economic relations, a system that responds readily to change and to changing needs, and one for which every nation will wish to claim ownership.

29

Give Developing Countries A More Favourable Deal:

An Assessment of the World Trade Conference in Doha

At the end of the 4th WTO Ministerial Conference in Doha, Qatar, the representatives of all WTO member states vigorously applauded Director-General Mike Moore when he dubbed the adopted work programmes for the new round of trade negotiations the "Doha development agenda."

The launching of a new round of trade negotiations with a broad agenda was the objective persistently pursued by the industrial countries, in particular the European Union, the United States, Canada and Japan. This objective has been achieved. Besides the continuation of the negotiations in the fields of agriculture and services, the Ministerial Declaration adopted by the Conference provides for the opening of negotiations in eleven additional fields. Undoubtedly a success for the industrial countries.

Clear Mandate for a New Development Round

The negotiating mandate, though, clearly reflects the political will to make the new round a "development round" with the aim of significantly improving the integration of the developing countries into the world trading system. To a large extent it takes into account the specific interests of the developing countries. Certainly a success with which the developing countries can credit themselves. A crucial factor for the course and the successful outcome of the Ministerial

Conference was, without doubt, the active involvement of the developing countries in the preparatory and negotiating process.

Doha Determines Merely the Work Programme for Negotiations

The Ministerial Declaration adopted at the conference merely determines the work programme for the new round of trade negotiations. Three factors contributed decisively to the positive outcome of the Ministerial Conference. There was a broad consensus among the WTO members states that (*i*) a second Seattle-like failure would put the WTO's workability at risk and was to be avoided at all costs (the 3rd WTO Ministerial Conference I Seattle in December 1999 ended in chaos without the adoption of a Ministerial Declaration); (*ii.*) the recessionary trends in the world economy were to be countered with the successful conclusion of the Ministerial Conference in Doha to improve the prospects for short-term recovery and, thereafter, sustained economic growth; (*iii.*) in response to the terrorist attacks of September 11, 2001, there should be a clear commitment to strengthen the rules-based multilateral trading system. Failure was, therefore, not an option, The strategic conclusion drawn from the Seattle failure was to limit the Doha Ministerial Declaration to establishing a broad, generally-worded negotiating mandate for a new round of trade talks that does not anticipate the outcome of the negotiations on controversial issues. The strategy worked. The deliberations at the Ministerial Conference focused on the scope of the negotiating mandate. The task of reconciling the conflicting interests between industrial and developing countries and working out a fair compromise has been left to the forthcoming negotiations.

Recognition of the Interests of the Developing Countries

In view of the objectives of creating a basis for sustained economic growth in the developing countries by better integrating them into the world economy and increasing their share in world trade, important preliminary decisions with regard to the forthcoming negotiations were taken by the Ministerial Conference:

- the Ministerial Declaration stresses the importance of implementing and interpreting the Agreement on Trade-Related Aspects of Intellectual Property Rights

(TRIPS Agreement) in a manner supportive of public health and access to medicines; in recognition of the seriousness of the problem, a separate 'Declaration on the TRIPS Agreement and Public Health' was adopted; a number of public-health related issues have been referred to the Council for TRIPS for further deliberation;

- the Council for TRIPs has been asked to examine the relationship between *(i,)* the TRIPS Agreement and the Convention on Biological Diversity and *(ii,)* the protection of traditional knowledge, taking full account of the development dimensions;
- numerous problems regarding the implementation of WTO agreements are dealt with in a separate 'Decision on Implementation-Related Issues and Concerns' adopted by the Ministerial Conference; outstanding implementation issues are to be addressed as a matter of priority by the relevant WTO bodies;
- the Council for Trade in Goods will examine the proposal to bring forward the liberalisation of the textile sector under the Agreement on Textiles and Clothing;
- as regards agriculture, comprehensive negotiations were agreed on, aiming at: substantial improvements in market access; reductions of, with a view to phasing out, all forms of export subsidies; and substantial reductions in trade-distorting domestic support;
- as regards market access for non-agricultural goods, negotiations were agreed on, with the aim of reducing or, as appropriate, eliminating tariffs and non-tariff trade barriers in particular on products of export interest to developing countries;
- recognition of the principle of special and differential treatment of the developing countries as an integral part of all WTO agreements;
- technical cooperation and capacity building have been recognised in the Ministerial Declaration as 'core

elements of the development dimension of the multilateral trading system' and firm commitments have been established in various paragraphs.

Turning the Ministerial Declaration's Spirit into Practical Policy

With these preliminary decisions regarding the agenda of the forthcoming negotiations, the course is set for the better integration of the developing countries into the world economy. To stay the course, there must be clear commitment and political will on the part of the industrial countries to make the new round a 'development round' by taking the developing countries' interest fully into account, being prepared to make meaningful concessions, and making good on the promise of significantly increased trade and investment-related technical assistance.

In the course of the negotiations it might prove a problem that many of the obligations in favour of the developing countries are formulated rather vaguely. The Ministerial Declaration is confined to declarations of intent even where—with a certain degree of goodwill—binding commitments would have been politically feasible. The bringing forward of the liberalisation of the textile sector, a key demand of the developing countries, has been referred to the Council for Trade in Goods for examination; this is certainly an expression of the industrial countries' willingness to compromise, but is in no way anticipates the final decision. As regards the objective of duty-free and quota-free access for all products of the least developed countries to the markets of the industrial countries the Ministerial Declaration simply repeats the commitment which was already expressed in the United Nations Millennium Declaration of September 2000, at the 3rd United Nations Conference on Least Developed Countries in Brussels in May 2001, and at the G7/8 Summit in Genoa in July 2001. Except for the European Union, no party has put this commitment into practice so far; the United States and Japan in particular have shown little enthusiasm for introducing duty-free and quota-free of all LDC products.

What makes us believe that the Doha Ministerial Declaration will make a difference? The chapter on agriculture is more specific in that it provides for negotiations aimed at significantly improved market access, reductions/phasing out of all forms of export subsidies, and substantial reductions in trade-distorting domestic support. However, a clear road map including a timetable for the negotiations and specific benchmarks for the reduction targets were beyond Doha's reach; in addition, the qualifier that the commitment to comprehensive negotiations does not prejudge the outcome of these negotiations leaves a back door open. In conclusion: If you remove the merely rhetorical phrases—such as "we place the developing countries' needs and interests at the heart of the World Programme adopted in this Declaration", "to take fully into account the development dimension...",—from the Ministerial Declaration, it becomes quite clear that the text contains relatively few 'programming elements' with a view to the development agenda of the forthcoming negotiations.

Fears that the vested interests of the industrial countries will re-gain precedence over development aspects in the course of the negotiating process are certainly not entirely baseless. The 'steel war' the United States is about to declare on the rest of the world clearly indicates that the Doha fair weather period is over. Business as usual has returned. The American steel tariff threats prompted EU Trade Commissioner Pascal Lamy to speak of a "perverse signal at a time when the ink is barely dry on the Doha Agreement."

The non-governmental organisations have a decisive role to play. It is their role to monitor the new round of trade negotiations, to make the negotiating process more transparent, to create public awareness with regard to the issues at stake, and to build up political pressure with the objective of making sure that development aspects are not pushed to one side and that the interest of the developing countries will makes their way into the agreements to be concluded.

Coherence of Trade Policy and Development Policy

The negotiating mandate for the new round of trade talks adopted in Doha has brought development politics onto the agenda of the WTO. The mention of development aspects in the WTO set of rules and regulations is not, in essence, new. In fact, the development dimension is recognized as an integral part of the general WTO mandate to foster economic growth. However, the particular importance the Doha Ministerial Declaration attaches to the consideration of development aspects in the negotiation process (it seeks, as it is put there, "to place the developing countries' needs and interests at the heart of the work programme") offers the opportunity to achieve greater coherence of trade policy and development policy. In this respect, the Doha Ministerial Declaration reflects the same trend as the "Everything-but-Arms-Initiative" (EBA) of the European Union. Subsequent to its adoption by the EU member states, Pascal Lamy emphasized the coherence aspect as the characteristic feature of EBA Initiative (outweighing the shortcomings relating to bananas, rice, and sugar) by saying, "It is the first time that the European Union's trade policy has been substantially modified by the necessity of contributing to development policy." This perspective also characterized the 3rd United Nations Conference on Least Developed Countries in Brussels in May 2001.

To sum up, it can be said that the Doha conference has sent out an important signal for the process of coordinating trade and development policy with the long-term objective of achieving a coherent policy framework. The next step towards greater coherency can be taken at the International Conference on Financing for Development in Monterrey/Mexico in March 2002.

Sustainable Development as the Guideline for Further Developing the Multilateral Trading System

The Ministerial Declaration reaffirms the commitment to the objective of sustainable development, as stated in the preamble to the Marrakesh Agreement of April 1994 (i.e. the Agreement establishing the WTO). However, theory and practice are far apart. The negotiating mandate for the new round is too cautious a step towards integrating environmental and social aspects into the WTO set of rules and regulations to be able to bridge that gap. Looking at the three pillar of the sustainable development concept—economic development, environmental protection, and social protection, in a nutshell the following can be said:

The negotiating mandate for the new round deserves good grades as far as the first pillar, economic development, is concerned. The course is set for better integration of the developing countries into the multilateral trading system, thus giving them the chance of actually benefiting from further trade liberalisation in the form of trade-induced economic growth. The inclusion of the so-called 'Singapore issues', investment and competition, offers the prospect of a medium to long-term improvement of the business and investment climate in the developing countries. As for environmental protection; negotiations on a (very) limited scale have been agreed on, the desirability of further negotiations will be examined. This is certainly not a big breakthrough, but a first step towards integrating ecological aspects into the trade rules. Disappointingly (but not surprisingly), social issues were not dealt with at the Doha Ministerial Conference. The developing countries' resistance to even discussing social issues, such as core labour standards, in the framework of the WTO could not be overcome; the issue was considered an absolute 'deal-breaker'.

Outlook

The developing countries' consent to the launching of a new round of trade talks cannot disguise the fact that there are still significant differences of opinion over a number of issues, including such key issues as agriculture, environment, investment and competition, and that there is a great deal of mistrust on the part of the developing countries. The one-day extension of the Ministerial Conference alone is proof of how difficult the process of reaching consensus on the launching of a new round of trade talks and its agenda had been. In order to successfully conclude the new round, the industrial countries have to deliver on their commitments, such as improving market access for goods of export interest to the developing countries and increasing their trade-related technical assistance.

The assurance of increased technical assistance was a major bargaining chip in getting the development countries' OK for the new round. If insufficient funds for technical assistance and capacity building measures are provided, it will most certainly diminish the chance of getting quick results. In a comment on the forth coming negotiations, the British Economist also highlighted the credibility aspect and the need for significant concessions, "Poor countries remain deeply suspicious of the rich world's commitment to truly freer trade. They bitterly remember the Uruguay Round, whose benefits went mostly to the rich. For the new talks to succeed, those suspicions must be proven wrong. Europe and America must quickly open up their markets for farm products and textiles. They must show that environmental concerns are not going to become a backdoor excuse for renewed protectionism. They must reform their oft-abused system of anti-dumping rules. And they must deliver on promises to beef up poorer countries' capacity to deal with the intricate procedures in the world trading system."

The Doha Ministerial Declaration offers the prospect of long-term gains for the developing countries. However, turning potential into actual gains requires tenacity in pursuing policies aimed at improving the business climate and, in general, the framework conditions for economic growth. Increased trade-related technical assistance and improved market access will not automatically result in growing export volumes for the developing countries. In addition, the strengthening and diversification of productive capacity is required. Successful integration into the global economy depends on tackling the supply-side constrains and other 'behind-the border impediments to trade' (ranging from weak infrastructure. Insufficient ancillary services and poor governance to macroeconomic instability). The Tanzanian Trade Minister, Iddi Simba, emphasized the complexity of the problems the developing countries are facing in his statement at the Ministerial Conference: "To operationalise the development agenda we need to have adequate capacity building which will go beyond addressing the normal WTO obligations. Adequate resources in the form of financial and technology transfer need to be in place to address the supply-side constraints. Along the same lines, WTO Director-General Mike Moore stated, "Capacity problems [in producing goods and services competitively], not trade barriers, are the major obstacles to growth in developing countries."

Concluding Remark

By creating a rules-based multilateral trading system, the WTO set of rules and regulations contributes to the shaping of the process of globalisation and to the emerging system of global governance. However, it can hardly be disputed that so far the industrial countries have been the main beneficiaries of the WTO-driven economic globalisation. We are still miles away from a true win-win situation. In a recent interview with the German weekly *Die Zeit, the,* Nigerian President, Olusegun Obasajo, criticized the industrial countries ' countries hypocrisy, saying "Globalisation is a good thing. Bu only if there is a level playing field, from which all countries are able to benefit. You tell us that we have to open up our markets for your goods, whereas you keep your markets closed for our goods. Europe protects itself with innumerable trade barriers, everybody know that. What kind rules are those?"

That is exactly what matters. The new round of trade negotiations lunched in Doha must result in modified trade rules. Trade rules which take account of the specific economic constraints of the developing countries and are more favourable to them. The developing countries must be given the chance to 'cash in' on trade liberalisation and, strengthened by trade-induced economic growth, to pursue national pro-poor policies aimed at eradicating poverty.

Bibliography

Books

Abdul Aziz, *The Rural Poor, Problems and Prospects,* Ashis Publishing House, New Delhi, 1983.

Arora R.C., *Industry and Rural Development,* S. Chand and Co Pvt. Ltd: 1978.

Alexander. R.J., *"A Primer to Economic Development"* The Macmillian and Co. Ltd. London 1962.

Barn, P.A., *Political Economy of Growth,* New York, 1962.

Behari Bepin, *Rural Industrialisation in India.* Vikas Publishing House Pvt. Ltd., New Delhi, 1976.

Battacharya S.N., *"Development of Industrial Backward Area"* (Indian Style) Metropolitan, Pragati Press; through V.R.N. Composing Agency, Delhi, 1981.

Bhojendra Nath Benerjee, *Industry, Agriculture and Rural Development,* B.R. Publishing Corporation, New Delhi, 1987.

Cykor. G., *Strategies for Industrialisation in Developing Countries,* C. Hurst and Co., London 1974.

Dandekar V.M., *Poverty in India,* New Delhi, the Ford Foundation, 55, Lodi House, 1970.

Desai Vasanth, *Problems and Prospects Small Scale Industries,* Himalaya Publishing House, Bombay 1983.

Eygene Staleey and Richard Morse; *Modern Small Scale Industry for Developing Countries,* Mc Graw Hill Book Co, New York 1965.

Francis Cherunilam, *"Industrial Economics Indian Perspective",* Himalaya Publishing House, Delhi, 1989.

Gunnar Myrdal, *"Economic Theory and Under Developed Regions"* Vora and Co. Publishing (P) Ltd. Bombay 1958.

Gunnar Myrdal, *"International Economy New York",* Happer and Brothers 1956.

Gandhi. M.K., *Village Industries*, Navajeevan Publishing House, Ahmedabad, 1960.

Kuchal. S.C., *Industrial Economy of India*, Chaitanya Publishing House, 1972, Ahmedabad-2.

Kalchetty Eresi, *Management of Finance in Small Scale Industries*, Vohra Publishers and Distributors, Allahabad, 1989.

Lakshman Rao, V., *"Economic Development of Andhra Pradesh"*, B.R. Publishing Corporatioin, Delhi 1985.

Madar. G.R. *India's Developing Villages*, Print House, Lucknow, 1978.

Mohanlal, *Rural Industrialisation and Regional Development*, New Delhi, Deep and Deeep Publication 1987.

Narasaiah. M.L., *Development of Small Scale Industries*, New Delhi, Discovery Publishing House, 1999.

Papola. T.S., *Rural Industrialisation Approaches and Potential*, Himalaya Publishing House, New Delhi. 1982.

Rao V.K.R.V., *Small Scale and Cottage Industries*, Chaitanya Publishing House, 1965.

Ramakrishna Sharma, *"Industrial Development of Andhra Pradesh"* Himalays Publishing House, Bombay 1982.

Sharma. D.P. and Desai. V.V., *"Rural Economy of India."* Vikar Publishing House Pvt. Ltd., Delhi, 1980.

Sarma. R.K., *Idustrial Development of Andhra Pradesh, A Regional Analysis*, Bombay, Himalaya Publisting House, 1982.

Sutchiffe. R.B., *Industry and Development*, Addison Wasley Publishing Co, London, 1971.

Sadak. H, *Industrial Development in Backward Regions in India*. Allahabad, Caught Publication, 1986,

Tarun. T.N.S., *Small Scale Industries and India Economic Development*, Deep and Deep Publication, New Delhi, 1986.

Vepa. Ram. K., *Small Industry in the Seventies*, Delhi, Vikash Publication, 1971.

Vepa. Ram. K., *How to Succeed in Small-Scale Industry*, New Delhi, Vikas Publishing House, 1984.

Articles

Anuradha. S.V., *Self Promoted Eco Friendly Industrial Production by the Masses. A Possibility or Dream*, Khadi-Gramodyoga, Vol. XXXXVI. No. 11, August 2000, Page 310.

Agarwall. A.K., *Agricultural Growth, Rural Industrialisation and Rural Development in India*, Khadi-Gramodyog, Vol No. XXXXVI. No. 12 p. 348.

Basheer Ahamed. F.M., *Sickness in Small Scale Industries an Over View, Southern Economist*, Vol. 38, No 18, January 15, 2000, p. 19.

Chellapan. K., *Tackling Mass Labour Unemployment in the New Era*, Khadi-Gramodyog, Vol XXXXVII No. 1, October 2000, p. 75.

Khan. A.V. and Zaqullah Shaik, *Southern Economist*, May 1, 2001, Vol. No. 40, Annual Number 1.

Moli P. Kosy and Mary Joseph, *Women Entrepreneurship in the Small Scale Industrial Units, A Case Study of Kerala, Southern Economist*, March 1, 20001, Vol. No. 39, Number 21, p. 19.

Dr. Prasad. C.S., *Special Attention to Small Scale Sector, Union Budget in 1999-2000* [Additional Development Commissioners & Economic Adviser Office of D.C. (SSI)]. Laghu Udyog Samachar, Development of S.S.I., A & R.I. Ministry of Industry, Government of India, January-March 1999, p.3.

Raju. S.V., *The Recent Environmental Changes and Impact on Small Scale Industrial Sector, Southern Economist*, April, 1 & 15, 2001, Vol. 39, Number 23 & 24, p.7.

Singh, M.P. Director (E.A.) O/o Development Commissioner (S.S.I.) Laghu Udyog Samachar, Development of S.S.I., A & R.I. Minstry of Industry Government of India, January-September 1988, p. 15.

Sheela Bhide, *Development of Small Scale Industries, Collaborative Approach, Economic and Political Weekly*, December 9, 2000, p. 4389.

Dr. Soundara Pandian, M., *District Industries Centre for Small Enterprise Development, Issues and Solution*, Kurukshetra, December 2000, p. 12.

Smt. Vasundara Raje, *The Role of S.S.I. in Promoting Economic Development, Southern Economist*, Vol. 39, Number 4, June 15, 2000, p. 11.

Smt. Vasundara Raje (Minister of State Independent Charge) Small Scale Industries Agro & Rural Industries, Government of India, *Taking S.S.I. Towards New Millenium Messages of Hope*, Laghu Udyog Samachar April-September 2000 Cover Story.

Valasmma Antony. M.S., "*Quarterly Economic Report, the Indian Institute of Public Opinion* New Delhi, Vol. 43, Number 4, October-December 2000, P. 172.

Umat. R.C. *The New Industries and Investment Policy*, Yojana, July 16-31, 1991, p.8.

Reports

Industrial Potential Survey Report of Kurnool District, Report Prepared by Commissioner of Industries, Hyderabad.

Government of Andhra Pradesh, *Statistical Abstract of Andhra Pradesh*, Hyderabad, Directorate of Economic & Statistics 1999-2000.

District Planning Office. *The Hand Book of Statistics Kurnool District*, Kurnool 1994-95.

Government of India, First Five Plan, Second Five Year Plan, Third Five Year Plan, Annual Plans, Fourth Five Year Plan, Fifth Five Year Plan, Sixth Five Year Plan, Seventh Five Year Plan, Eighth Five Year Plan and Ninth Five Year Plan.

Index

T

U

V

W

Z